A PLACE BEYOND

A PLACE BEYOND

Finding Home in Arctic Alaska

NICK JANS

ALASKA NORTHWEST BOOKS®

For my parents

❖

Library of Congress Cataloging-in-Publication Data
Jans, Nick, 1955–
    A place beyond : finding home in Arctic Alaska / Nick Jans.
        p.   cm.
    ISBN 978-0-88240-807-1 (alk. paper)
    1. Kobuk River Region (Alaska)—Description and travel.   2. Eskimos—Alaska—Kobuk River Region—Social life and customs.   3. Kobuk River Region (Alaska)—Social life and customs.   4. Eskimos—Alaska—Ambler—Social life and customs.   5. Ambler (Alaska)—Social life and customs. 6. Homes and haunts—Alaska—Ambler.   I. Title.
F912.K6J37   1996
979.8'6—dc20   96-19763
                                                                          CIP

Designer: Elizabeth Watson
Map: Vikki Leib and Elizabeth Watson
Cover Design: Vicki Knapton

Photographs: All photos are by the author.

Alaska Northwest Books®
An imprint of Turner Publishing Company
507 Charlotte Avenue, Suite 100
Nashville, TN 37209
(615) 255-2665
www.turnerbookstore.com

CONTENTS

ACKNOWLEDGMENTS

I offer heartfelt thanks to the following people: to Lynn and Carol Norstadt, who read everything twice; to Jennifer Maler, good friend and literary advisor nonpareil; to Marlene Blessing and Ellen Wheat, whose tireless work is behind this; to Steve and Venita Pilz, who were always home; to Ken, Tricia, and the gang at *ALASKA* magazine, who cheered me on. Thanks also to Cindy Horsfall, who helped arrange the manuscript.

I'm most deeply indebted to my Eskimo friends Clarence Wood and Minnie Gray, and to all the Ambler people. One word says it all: *Taiikuu.*

BROOKS RANGE

Ambler

ALASKA

PREFACE

One bright April morning a dozen years ago, Clarence Wood and I stood on the crest of a birch knoll, looking out over the upper Kobuk valley. Before us, thousands of caribou grazed, dark specks trailing off into the blue-white distance. Clarence turned, his weathered Eskimo face split by a wide grin. "Lots," he said quietly. "Lots."

The longer I live here and write, the more I find myself following Clarence's cue—turning to simpler words, and fewer of them. My hope, in these twenty-eight brief essays about life in the Alaskan arctic, is to find words not big enough, but small enough for a landscape and a place without end.

Grandpa's Ghost

❖

Seventeen years ago, I slammed the door of my grandfather's '66 Plymouth Belvedere and headed for Alaska. He'd died the year it was new, before I'd gotten a chance to really know him, but the car had stayed in the family and eventually been passed down to me. As I rattled five thousand miles across the continent, pistons wheezing and bearings grumbling, I told myself that Grandpa Paul would have approved. The son of an immigrant, he'd have known why I'd shoved my last four hundred bucks in my pocket and fled from a future that looked all too certain.

Of course, I was coming back. Everyone waved cheerfully as I drove off, canoe strapped to the roof of what I privately called Grandpa's Ghost.

The questions started a year later. "When are you coming home?" my father asked, his voice echoing over the satellite phone. A retired career diplomat, he could fathom the lure of distant places, but not the idea of his son pricing canned beans in an Eskimo village store. My mother, intuitive and theatrical, came closer to understanding. But she wanted to know when, too.

"I don't know. Next year," I said, believing the sound of my own voice. But a year became five, then ten. Even though I was now teaching English, history, and math in the Ambler school, putting my education to good use and getting paid for it, my parents' questions never quite stopped. What was I doing up there, hauling water in buckets and peeing in an outhouse? When was I going to get on with my life?

The real question, though, wasn't what or when, but why. I knew they didn't quite understand what held me here. If only they could sit with me and watch the caribou flowing south down the Redstone valley, or smell the tundra after a late spring rain. Come up, I told them, and I'll show you.

Two summers ago, my mother, father, and sister-in-law Kate stood outside my boarded-up cabin as I fumbled with the padlock. The late July day was warm and still; mosquitoes buzzed lazily in the fireweed. We'd been traveling together for three weeks, driving from Oregon to Prince Rupert, then the ferry to Skagway, on to Whitehorse, and up the highway to

Anchorage and Fairbanks—two thousand miles and change.
We'd done all the usual tourist drill: sea otters and eagles...
check; cheap souvenirs...check; Alaska Railroad...check; grizzlies, moose, and mountains...check. The postcard version of
Alaska, most of which I'd never seen, was all interesting and
pretty enough.

Okay, spectacular at times. I was just as excited as anyone
when a whale rolled fifty yards off the ferry's bow. Resurrection
Bay was good, too. At Denali Park, we spotted more critters
out of a bus window than I'd be likely to see in a week up
north. But all the time I was restless, and my parents felt it. All
this scenery, grand as it was, explained nothing about where I
lived, or why.

Now we were home, three hundred miles from the nearest
Princess Tour. "There's the outhouse behind that tree," I
pointed. "And this bucket here is for drinking water." The
familiar, comforting shapes of the Jade Mountains shone blue
in the evening sun. Crossbills twittered in the trees.

My mother and father nodded quietly. There in the path
lay a caribou leg bone, hoof and all. A four-wheeler roared by,
trailing dust. "Tell me," my father said, "why you live in the
middle of all this trash." He gestured toward the oil barrels, the
snowmobile carcasses behind the woodpile. I tried to explain.
Tight, clean fuel drums were a commodity, and there were
good parts on those machines. Trash? This was wealth.

Kate and Mom cleaned while I unboarded windows, split
wood. There were dozens of small chores, and everyone

pitched in. It felt good to be working with my hands again. This was more like it, I thought. They're smiling. They like it here.

Later on, my neighbors Lynn and Carol told me how Mom and Dad had confided in them. Though they found everyone here more than friendly, they thought my cabin was filthy and cluttered, the bed lumpy, my lifestyle primitive. What had gone wrong? They hadn't raised their son to live this way.

So much for the village. Out in the country, things would be different. I'd envisioned all of us soaring up the Ambler River in my new jetboat—just us, the caribou, and the Brooks Range. No crowds of New York tourists looking over our shoulders, no bogus guide chattering away. We'd camp on a gravel bar forty miles from anyone, catch grayling from water clear as air, hear wolves howling at twilight. Then they'd understand.

My new boat, however, bought and paid for months ago, hadn't arrived in Kotzebue yet. I'd figured to fly down and drive it back the first day. Instead, we were stuck in Ambler, waiting. The week we'd planned up here was melting away. It wasn't supposed to go like this.

We never did make it back into the mountains. Instead, we settled for a day trip to Minnie Gray's fish camp in a borrowed boat, thirty miles up the broad, dull Kobuk. A nice enough outing, but hardly what I'd pictured. We caught a few hammer-handle pike, drank coffee with Minnie and Sarah, and watched them cut fish. On the ride home, my parents shivered in the wind. Though they didn't complain once, I knew they were ready to go home.

I ended up spending the next two days in Kotzebue, waiting for my boat. Meanwhile, my parents were back in Ambler, meeting my friends, both white and Eskimo, telling them stories of their son's childhood, reliving a time when we knew each other.

The two-hundred-mile ride upriver to Ambler took another day, and I walked in the door just in time to wave good-bye. We smiled and hugged at the gravel airstrip; Kate, who'd spent three days working at Minnie's fish camp, was radiant. My parents looked tired.

As I watched, the little plane faded into the sky, headed toward Fairbanks, where fifteen years ago I'd parked Grandpa's Ghost on a back road, put it up on blocks, and walked off into a new life. I'd like to think the car's still there; I suspect someone hauled it off for junk. But if Grandpa could see where his ghost carried me, maybe he'd smile and nod.

Putyuq Always Get

❖

Not too good," Clarence Wood murmurs to me. He and Elwood Brown stand looking at the sky, conversing quietly in Inupiaq. A dark line of clouds is rising from the southeast, shouldering against the Waring Mountains.

"Snow?" I ask hopefully.

"Rain," says Clarence.

"Rain for sure," says Elwood. He grins and shrugs as if it's no big deal, but I know better. A half hour ago, both he and Clarence were asleep in our duck blind, resting up after last night's hunt; now they're gathering tarps, geese, and gear, loading their sleds with quiet urgency. I take my cue and join in. We're twenty miles from Ambler, and the trail home is collapsing.

In the upper Kobuk, from the end of April on, traveling by snowmobile is an increasingly iffy proposition. Now, in mid-May, the tundra is a quagmire of slush and standing water; the river ice is rotting away, turning black under the arctic sun. It might still be four feet thick, but where the current swirls, there are invisible thin spots and holes that can swallow you. Then there's overflow: sheets of water running on top of the ice, sometimes several feet deep. A warm day or two, a good rain, and the river will break up.

We know all that, but we're out here anyway. Water at this time of year means ducks and geese—Canadas, specklebellies, pintails, widgeons, and mallards winging north by the thousands. Most won't stay long; they're heading for their nesting grounds on the North Slope. This is the time to hunt, a two-week window before they're gone. Sinking your machine now and then is part of the deal. All up and down the Kobuk, Eskimo hunters are taking the same chances, all for a pot of duck soup, rich with fat.

I'm a little edgy about going out this far, this late in the season, but I trust Clarence. He's been doing this late-season stuff longer than I've lived, first with dogs, the last twenty-five years with machines. On the other hand, I've also been up to my waist in ice water following him, and broken down at forty below. But he always makes it home, usually with his sled groaning with meat—caribou, geese, bear, moose—most of which he gives away in the village.

"Putyuq always get," the Ambler people say, using his Eskimo name, and nod their approval.

This time, though, we may have pushed our luck too far. We were counting on a cold, clear evening to freeze things up a bit; driving down last night, we rode a crust of new ice. Even so, Clarence, Elwood, and I all plowed into overflow at Siglioruk, where the trail swings from the tundra onto the main river. Grunting and shoving, ice water lapping at the tops of our waders, we'd managed to keep our engines above the slush. It took almost an hour to cross a hundred yards to solid ice.

Then we'd gone on, to the tip of Onion Portage, where the Kobuk doubles back on itself. "Right here," Clarence motioned to a willowy gravel bar with a shallow, half-open slough in its lee. We built our blind from brush and burlap, and settled down to wait. Elwood brought out coffee, and Clarence asked, "Where's your stove?"

I'd agreed to bring my little Coleman, but it had sprung a leak. Instead, I borrowed Lynn and Carol's MSR, a spidery, high-tech miniature that Clarence had never seen. He and Elwood stood dumbfounded as I pumped up and lit the tiny burner.

Finally Elwood muttered, "What the shit?"

Clarence shook his head. "Sometimes I don't know about you white people."

The first birds came flying before dawn. Elwood and Clarence knocked down a couple of pintails, then a specklebelly,

and I propped them up as decoys. Small bunches came steadily;
I kept warm by retrieving. Every now and then I'd take a shot,
but I wanted only a couple of geese. There was plenty of time.
Clarence and Elwood swung and fired, seldom missing.

Sometime before noon, the action stopped. The sun beat
down until the snow shimmered with heat waves. Songbirds
twittered in the willows; Clarence and Elwood answered them
with snores. Drowsy, I wandered down the bar, found a patch
of warm sand, and took off my shirt. Somewhere across the
tundra, sandhill cranes squawked like giant rusty hinges, the
doors of summer swinging open.

When I'd returned to the blind, sunburned and shivering
in the late afternoon, Clarence and Elwood were just coming to.

"You could make coffee?" Elwood grinned, motioning
toward my cartoon stove.

A half hour later we're riding for home, chased by those
dirty clouds. Since I'm not pulling a sled, it's my job to lead—
about as much of an honor as being point man on a Vietnam
jungle patrol. Leaning forward in the flat light, I strain to keep
on our incoming trail. But everything has changed. On the first
sandbar, the snow has evaporated. Where we'd left the river, a
twenty-yard patch of ice has caved in. Ahead, sheets of overflow glisten where there had been solid going. But there's no
choice for the next few miles; it's the river or nothing.

By the time we reach Siglioruk, I'm soaking wet and my
nerves are shot. Half a dozen times I've felt the sickening lurch
of ice giving way, and have just kept afloat by gunning the

throttle wide open. Twice I've backtracked to help Clarence and Elwood, mired to the thigh in blue-green slush. But we've kept our engines above water—always the big issue—and avoided the serious holes. Now, just ahead, lies two hundred yards of freezing slop, with a dark, open lead against the bank. All we have to do is get across and we'll be on tundra the last twelve miles.

"What you figure, Clarence?" I ask, knowing the answer.

"Well, just have to drive like hell," he shrugs. I turn, circle to get up speed, and hydroplane across the channel, engine howling. But it's no use. Clarence and Elwood's sleds, heavy with birds, have bogged down again. I have to go back.

Clarence throws me a rope. With the two machines yoked together, we make solid ground in a roar of spray. Then I go back for Elwood. Fifteen wet minutes later, we're all across.

"Not too bad," says Clarence, lighting a cigarette as I shiver, dumping slush from my waders. "Maybe I'll come back tomorrow."

Thin Water

❖

One June day sixteen years ago, my friend Peter and I stood on the shores of Walker Lake, listening as the floatplane's roar faded into the sky. Mounds of gear lay scattered around us, along with the canoe that would take us seven hundred miles in the next two months: down the Kobuk from the headwaters, up the Ambler and over Natmaktugiaq Pass into the Noatak, and downstream to Kotzebue on the Chukchi Sea. For me, ten days new to Alaska, it seemed the canoe trip of a lifetime.

It still does. Though I've traveled thousands of river miles since, I haven't taken a fly-in, float-out trip in fourteen years, and don't know when I will. As a matter of fact, I can't remember the last time I paddled a canoe. No, wait. It was in Maine, visiting my parents two summers ago.

Face it, in arctic bush Alaska, canoes are for "floaters," as the Inupiat call the tourists who travel thousands of miles to play at what The People once did in earnest. Come to think of it, I don't know one Eskimo in the northwest arctic who owns either a canoe or a kayak, though there must be a few.

On the other hand, every family has at least one outboard-powered boat. All eleven villages in the region are on navigable rivers or the coast. From breakup in June to freezeup in October, motorboats are part of daily life, and in a land without roads, rivers take the place of highways. Women make regular runs to fish camp or out berry picking, and the young men hunt beaver, moose, bear, and ducks in season. Entire families travel huge distances, often hundreds of miles, between summer camps on the coast and inland villages. Coastal Eskimos range far out to sea in search of seals, then converge in the fall at the caribou crossings up the Noatak and Kobuk. A round trip of a hundred miles in an aluminum skiff pushed by twenty-five-horsepower "motors" is a trifling matter, hardly worth mentioning.

Though I first came to Ambler in a canoe, I soon learned the damn thing was almost worthless. Paddling upstream was a career, and if you floated down, how would you get back? The country started on your doorstep, and without a motor, you were a prisoner. My canoe ended up rotting on the bank.

It just wasn't enough in a place so big that twenty miles meant nothing.

My first real boat was a leaky wooden skiff that I bought for fifty bucks, with an equally decrepit Johnson eighteen-horse sagging off the stern. The motor crapped out with astounding regularity. It was, in local parlance, strictly an "upstream" rig. You always headed upriver so that when, not if, you broke down, the current took you home. But at least I got out past the hum of the village generator, and caught a few grayling.

Two years later, I had a brand-new Johnson 35 on a plywood speedboat, and was ranging three hundred miles. I was living in Noatak village by then, on the river of the same name—a shallow, rocky maze winding far into the western Brooks Range. Propeller-driven boats weren't made with water like this in mind, and my equipment took a steady beating, as everybody's did.

I was getting pretty good at reading channels, shoals, and eddies, but the places I most wanted to go were still out of reach—far up tributaries, often little more than creeks, where the water was transparent, the mountains were close enough to touch, and people just didn't go, at least not by boat.

Outboard jet units, I read, were the answer. No one I knew had one, but the idea was straightforward enough: you used the same boat, the same motor, but instead of a gearcase and prop that hung down in harm's way, you had a bolt-on turbine that lay almost flush with the bottom of the boat, sucked water in, and rammed it out to provide thrust. At full tilt, the brochure said, you could whiz through three inches of water. I plunked down my thousand bucks.

Of course, there was a catch or two. Though the contraption could run as shallow as they claimed, there was no guarantee against beating your boat to pieces, and you traded about half your power. With a good load—thirty gallons of gas, camping gear, and two people—I had to check the bank to see if I was making headway against the current. My Eskimo friends laughed. Just another *naluaqmiut* (white people) gadget. What good was a boat that couldn't carry a few caribou?

After twenty thousand bucks' worth of experiments with escalating horsepower and shredded boat bottoms, I figured things out. Most recently I've settled on a welded aluminum sixteen-footer with an inboard 115 jet, stripped down and modified for serious long-distance work.

It's still not perfect (no jetboat is ever fast enough, strong enough, or light enough), but I'm getting there. Last summer and fall I covered close to four thousand miles, most of those up remote tundra valleys hugging the Noatak divide.

These runs, a hundred to three hundred miles each, start off casually enough. But as side creeks drop away, narrowing the channel, and the mountains shoulder in, the driving gets more technical. With an almost flat bottom and no prop to grab water, a jetboat is about as stable as a '66 Mustang on glare ice. Turn the wheel a hair too far, and you spin out, plowing into rocks or cutbanks. And still you need to shuck and jive like an NFL running back, screaming over riffles that are little more than wet sand, hitting slots three feet wide.

The water keeps getting thinner, the chances bigger. Finally the whole world funnels down to a series of split-second moves, as visceral as some big, high-stakes video game. At the same time, there's the aesthetic thrill of body, boat, and river moving together, raw power and grace joined in delicate balance, like horse and rider. The insistent roar of machinery fades, ceases to matter somehow.

With gravel blurring by inches below my feet, fish scattering like birds, the mountains rising close on both sides, I'm often overwhelmed by the notion that gravity and time have fallen away. Just one more bend, I tell myself. Ahead, the country stretches into forever. I'm almost there.

Sometimes Always Never

❖

Once people find out I live in an Eskimo village, the questions begin. How cold is it? Do they live in igloos? What the hell are you doing there? Of course they want to know, and I do my best to fill in the blanks.

Sooner or later, someone asks, "Do you speak the language?"

"Sure do," I reply.

"Say something."

"I just did." My answer isn't complete, but it's the truth. In the village stores, in the gym, while visiting friends or fixing snowmachines, the majority of Inupiat—in other words, those under thirty—speak English.

Sort of. An outsider would have a tough time following along. A typical bit of dialog between two young adults might go like this:

"Where you was go?"

"Store. Next us."

"I should *malik, ah?*"

(Raised eyebrows in reply.)

"*Alappaa* your hands?"

(Slight squint in response.)

A quick fill-in: "us" means our house; *malik* means to follow; *ah* is a question word; raising eyebrows means yes, squinting, no; *alappaa* means cold.

Welcome to Village English: a polyglot built from two unrelated languages, stretched over a grammatical and cultural framework borrowed from both, with a few nonverbal cues thrown in. Fluid, poetic, utilitarian, logical in its illogic, Village English is the lingua franca of the northwest arctic—created to suit the needs of its users, and constantly adapted as new needs arise.

It was born just under a century ago, with the arrival of the first missionaries, miners, and traders. As *naluaqmiut* and Inupiat struggled to communicate, each picking up simple words from the other, the fine points of grammar, syntax, and vocabulary were tossed aside, casualties of the need to build a linguistic bridge between two cultures that had almost nothing in common.

Maybe, under more gradual and egalitarian circumstances, English and Inupiaq might have merged to form an entirely new language, the way Latin blended with tribal dialects to create English. But there was nothing gradual or egalitarian about the cultural exchange that went on. The Inupiat flocked to English-speaking missions, trading posts, mining camps, and schools, not the other way round. Most newcomers picked up just enough Inupiaq to get by.

Learning English was widely seen as a good thing, a way to get ahead in the new order. Adults sent their kids to the mission schools, and speaking Inupiaq—a complex, expressive language in its own right—became, almost overnight, something to be ashamed of. Few flinched when teachers handed out punishments to backsliders.

What emerged from this process, however, wasn't exactly Queen's English. Translations were difficult, especially when the teachers and missionaries had, at best, a hazy knowledge of Inupiaq.

And, as Ruthie Sampson, the bilingual coordinator for the region's schools, notes, "The grammatical structure of Inupiaq is 180 degrees from English, further removed than Chinese." Technically speaking, Inupiaq relies on a postbase construction: you start out with nouns and verbs, and add on series of descriptors (the rough equivalent of adjectives and adverbs) after the base word—thus, postbase. The descriptors aren't independent but directly linked to the base to form single word-phrases that are often longer than the entire English alphabet. The exact sequence of postbases is determined by rules so subtle they puzzle trained linguists.

Also, certain concepts *just don't translate*—the linguistic equivalent of not being able to get there from here. For example, "big," a simple adjective in English, is a descriptive *verb* in Inupiaq. You can translate the word, but not the idea of what "big" really is. The languages reflect radically different ways of looking at the world, especially when it comes to time and space. Village English phrases like "sometimes always" and even "sometimes always never" might be partially rooted in translation errors made long ago, but I think they also reflect the failure of standard English to express Inupiaq concepts.

Yeah, "sometimes always never" means something. I'm not sure exactly what, but it goes something like this: "Always" in Village English means "generally" or "habitually" (example: You always hunt wolf?); "sometimes always" roughs out as "occasionally"; "sometimes always never," as in "Sometimes I always never go there," gets watered down into "once in a blue moon." I suspect these phrases translate much more readily into Inupiaq. English, as a reflection of Anglo-Saxon culture, is much too linear and rational to make the necessary leap into wholesale paradox.

As you might expect, the patterns of Village English reflect those of Inupiaq. For example, nouns can easily become verbs, and vice versa. Someone can hand you a wrapped gift at Christmas and say, "I present you." An old man, frustrated by a mechanical problem, mutters, "This snogo too much problem me."

The most noticeable characteristic of Village English, though, is the way it scorns structural fluff. All but the most basic prepositions are scarce, and articles virtually absent, along with adverbs. Adjectives are simple, and kept to a minimum. Verb tenses don't count for much. Usually people use the present tense, and you figure out when by context.

All this isn't something you learn overnight. I spent my first year or two getting laughed at. You do need to know at least the few dozen words of Inupiaq that everyone uses, and there are patterns and colloquialisms to master. I guess you could say I'm fluent in Village English, but I feel foolish admitting that no, I can't really speak Eskimo. Then again, neither can half the village.

Meanwhile, Inupiaq is still the language of choice among people over forty. The problem is, too few children are learning too few words. Television, school, and friends exert an overwhelming influence, and forty minutes of Inupiaq class a day just isn't enough. Unless something drastic is done, Inupiaq will fade out as a living language in the next two generations. A full-scale language immersion program for preschoolers might work, but it needs to begin now. Always has already faded to sometimes. Never is just around the corner.

Gearhead Heaven

❖

I could smell something burning—a bad sign when you're riding a snowmobile. I told myself it must be a twig smoldering on the muffler, maybe the drive belt slipping a little. In the upper Noatak valley, five below zero and one hundred twenty-five miles from home, denial sets in fast.

But when my basket sled lugged down in less than a foot of snow and wouldn't budge, it was time to face reality. Bert, who'd been following a quarter mile back, pulled up.

"What's going on?"

"Fried bearing." Mentally I whacked myself. I'd gone through the machine from top to bottom the week before, as I always do before a long trip. The bearings had been due for a change, but, deciding to save two hours of wrench work (I had plenty to do already), I figured they'd last. Now it was pay-back time.

Rummaging around in my sled, I found my repair box— forty pounds of junk, everything from idler wheels to baling wire—and, I fervently hoped, drive-shaft bearings. Sure enough, there at the bottom. Now, two questions: was that really the trouble, and could I fix it?

A bearing job is no big deal at home, in a warm shop with all your tools handy. If something else is broken, or you're missing a part, you can shrug and make a phone call. Squatting on the Midas Creek flats was another story. Bert and I could limp back on one machine, but leaving the other this far out in the country would be bad news—a rough three-day trip just to come back and get the thing, if we could even find it.

My fingers already stiffening, I jimmied off the chaincase cover. Sure enough, both bearings were shot. But where was the hex wrench I needed to loosen the bearing collars? One hundred twenty-five miles away. Somehow we managed, improvising as we went. An hour later, we were on the trail again. Before we made home, though, we had to patch a sled hitch and tinker with a bad coil wire. Just another trip.

I wasn't raised to be Mr. Fixit. As a teenager, I owned a procession of junk cars, but my older brother Tony did all the real work. He was a gearhead, one of these guys who fondles flywheels and pistons. Changing oil was always enough of a thrill for me.

When I moved to arctic Alaska, I thought I was leaving all that stuff behind. Trading in modern appliances and cars for a log cabin had to be simpler. How was I to know I'd stumble into gearhead heaven? Everything out here rests on the shoulders of machinery. A chainsaw cuts down the tree that makes the cabin, and a snowmachine or outboard motor hauls it home. Then there are ATVs, generators, pumps, power tools, and who knows what. Sure, you can live without all that clutter, about as well as you'd live in L.A. without a car.

But the real catch is, there's no one around to fix things when they break. You can ship a snowmachine to a shop in Kotzebue for a few hundred bucks—one way—and there are a couple guys in Ambler you could hire. But what if your outboard quits out in the country? Besides, there's an unwritten code in bush Alaska: if you own it and you run it, you fix it. Getting advice is fine, and you can accept help without shame; but hiring or asking someone to do what you should do yourself is, at best, feebleminded behavior. People will talk behind your back.

And so I got sucked into the world of torque wrenches and crankshaft seals, just as surely as I learned to hunt or pitch a wall tent. I started out small, a single chainsaw and one snowmobile, fumbling over repairs and hating every minute.

Fifteen years later, I own a jetboat, four snowmobiles, an ATV, three chainsaws, three sleds, and a trailer, and every damn one needs work right now. These gadgets aren't like cars, where routine maintenance means checking the oil. After two seasons of serious use—anywhere from four to ten thousand miles—they start falling apart. Even the most solid are little more than toys built for the Lower 48 recreational market. As beasts of burden, hauling huge loads over long distances in the worst conditions, of course they disintegrate. A partial list of my current headaches: broken axle on the trailer; snapped throttle cable, broken choke lever, and dead battery on the ATV; splintered rails on one sled, cracked hitch on another; shot idler wheels and an electrical short on a snowmachine... I could go on, but you get the idea.

It seems I'm always working on something, parts, bolts, and tools strewn around the cabin, grease jammed under my nails. I spent two solid weeks this summer unraveling dozens of mechanical tangles. But I never quite got caught up, and can't remember when I have been. I just do the best I can, and hope a saw or snowmobile is running when I need it. Sometimes I run out of spares.

When I'm not fiddling around, I'm waiting for parts. You call dealers hundreds, even thousands, of miles away, and wait. Sometimes days, sometimes weeks, chewing your nails while the caribou pass without you, or the sheefish run hits its peak.

I try to stay ahead of the breakdown curve, replacing equipment every two or three years. Matter of fact, I bought both a brand-new boat and a snowmachine this year. I've already spent dozens of hours and hundreds of dollars patching them up, and had an entire engine replaced on warranty. This wasn't cheap junk, either. It was *expensive* junk. I could have bought a new car instead and pocketed the change. But where the hell would I go in a car?

Don't get me wrong. I'm not whining. I spend hours leafing through parts catalogs and shop manuals, and confess I sometimes catch myself musing about exhaust manifolds. I have long, intense conversations with total strangers about clutch calibration. I lust secretly after tools I don't yet own.

Alaska changes people, and I guess I'm no exception. I could say living here made me self-sufficient, opened my eyes to the natural world, taught me appreciation for Native culture. But more than anything else, living in the bush taught me to turn a wrench. And love it.

One of Us

❖

We buried John Blower today, out on the birch knoll above Ambler, among the people he knew. The tiny cemetery, less than a dozen wooden crosses, lies on the shoulder of the Jade Mountains, facing out over the blue-white stretch of the Kobuk valley. About a hundred of us stood in the snow, taking turns with the shovels, talking in low voices, listening to the clatter of frozen dirt on the coffin as the evening light faded. There were no undertakers, no hearse, no priest, no relatives; just his friends and neighbors standing together in the cold.

He came home to die. Sixty-three years old, struggling with emphysema, he'd been in and out of the veterans hospital in Fairbanks for years. Doctors had told him a decade ago that he had a few months to live, but he fooled them all. Each time they'd written him off he'd rallied and headed back to Ambler, to his cluttered frame house, his summer vegetable garden, and his two little mongrels, Pup and Shadow.

John had lived here since the '60s, when, just out of the army, he drifted into the upper Kobuk country. No one remembers how he ended up here or exactly why he came. Ambler, a tiny, newly settled Eskimo community, wasn't even on most maps. It was a place rooted in the past, where people depended on dog teams, hunted caribou, trapped and fished, and the mail plane came once a week, perhaps. John Blower, a wiry little man with a laconic, self-effacing sense of humor, rumpled shirt, and a mouthful of snuff, found a home among the *Iviisaapaatmiut* (Ambler people), and more: they elected him mayor or councilman several times, and he wrote the grants that helped the settlement of Ambler become—technically, at least—a city.

But in recent years, John's civic involvement had waned, and his trips to the hospital had become more frequent. Even when he was home he was seldom out, and few people visited him; it was easy to forget that he lived here at all. Once in a while I'd run into him at the post office, wheezing up the stairs, so frail that he seemed almost transparent. This winter he was gone for months. Then, one evening about a week ago,

John Blower landed at the gravel runway, caught a ride down the hill, unlocked his door, patted his dogs, lay down on his bed, and quietly died. He must have been hanging on, willing himself to make it home one last time.

In Ambler, as in any Eskimo village, a death involves the entire community. Nearly everyone is related, and the extended family pulls together for the funeral, sparing no expense, shrugging off inconvenience to make a proper display of respect and affection. Even distant cousins and *atiins*—those sharing the same first name—feel obligation, and may travel thousands of miles to attend. But John had no family here, had never married. He wasn't a member of the local Friends Church. After all these years, he was still somewhat of an outsider, as far as the Native community was concerned. His nearest kin, two elderly brothers and a sister, were five thousand miles away in Ohio, and didn't have the money or health to make the trip. There was no one to make the normal arrangements, not even enough money for a coffin. The *Iviisaapaatmiut* shook their heads when they heard no relatives were coming. How could that be? What was wrong with those *naluaqmiut* anyway?

Then Dave and Kaye Rue, part of the small white community, donated plywood to build a casket. John's friends for over twenty years, they assumed the role of family. Everyone understood, and the village, moving as one, swung into motion. Calls went out over the CB radio, and the various funeral committees, organized through the Friends Church, went to work. The coffin makers brought their tools to the old community hall, while others dug the grave, carved the marker, washed and dressed the body, collected donations, and cooked for the workers. Calls went out to Kotzebue for the Catholic priest, and he agreed to fly in for the service.

Although it was early May, a blizzard swept in, followed by another. No planes could fly. The funeral was delayed one day, then three. Meanwhile, John lay dead in his house. Even in the cold, the unembalmed body was starting to decay. People murmured about the smell. The service would have to be held, priest or no.

Outside the old log church, John's dogs, Pup and Shadow, sat and howled along as the bell tolled. The people of Ambler, white and Eskimo, filed in and sat together on the rickety wooden pews, dressed in their parkas and coveralls. The handmade coffin, surprisingly beautiful and fine, rested on sawhorses below the pulpit, draped with artificial flowers. I'd expected the place to be almost empty and the service to be short, even a bit awkward. But the church was nearly full. Ed Iten, a local dog musher and the only other Catholic in town, read haltingly through the service for the dead; the priest had coached him over satellite phone. When he was done, Kaye Rue gave the obituary. Pup and Shadow snuck in twice to sit by the coffin and had to be put out. All together the service lasted less than fifteen minutes. It wasn't much, but we'd done our duty, and could put the body to rest in good conscience.

Almost as an afterthought, Ed asked if anyone had something to add, and one by one, people came forward:

Jim Wilson, who told how John had helped him get started in commercial fishing; Wallace Cleveland, who reminded everyone of John's years of work for the community; and then a line of others, all speaking of John and what he'd done for them. Old Cora Cleveland spoke at length in Inupiaq, and then translated. "He was one of us," she said, and nodded. "One of us." Ed Iten, freed of his formal obligation, gave a short, eloquent speech about John's missing the wild geese this spring, and our missing him. As we sat in the drafty church singing "Amazing Grace," everyone understood. John's family had come after all.

A State of Mind

❖

From the edge of a sawtooth ridge, I peered down into the Redstone valley. The June day had begun bright and windswept, but now an overcast was drifting in from the east. Better get a move on, I thought. Camp was still two miles down the hill. As I slung my pack onto my shoulders, a big arctic mosquito thudded against my cheek. There had been a few through the day, but it was early in the season—the ice had gone out just two weeks before—and I'd scarcely noticed them. But now, as I wound down the ridge, the last breeze faded, and they were on me. Rising in clouds from the soggy tundra, they pelted against my face. I reached in my pocket for the repellent, and came up empty. In my shirt? Nope. The pack? Nothing. I was flailing away, nailing five or six at a whack, but there were a couple thousand mobbing me now. One swarm attacked low, while another squadron strafed my ears and neck. There was no dainty humming about, no fickle flitting. They were diving in nose first and tanking up, nailing me right through my clothes, dozens at a time. Four hands wouldn't have been enough. Years of Alaskan experience had taught me what to do in a situation like this. I turned up my collar, cinched my pack straps tight, and ran like hell.

When I saw the tent, I was still going strong. So were the bugs. I'd left the first swarm behind somewhere up the mountain, but there were more waiting every step of the way, and they trailed me in a whining veil. Each time I slowed, the mugging resumed. Pausing just long enough to unzip the screen door, I dove through to safety. It took me fifteen minutes to hunt down the hundred or so that made it inside with me.

After I'd cornered the last one, I took stock and tried to relax. My hands and neck were smeared with blood, and every inch of exposed skin was a cordillera of welts. At least I still had my wallet.

Outside, the insistent, lustful wail was nearly deafening. Mosquitoes settled over the tent, pattering on the nylon like rain. Though my grub box was just twenty yards away, I settled for the granola bars in my pack and a few swigs of stale water.

As I ate, they clustered on the windows, snouts probing hopefully through the mesh. I amused myself for a while by holding
my arm just a quarter inch out of reach as bait, then snipping
off proboscises with my Swiss army knife scissors. Not until
later that night, when a cold rain swept in and scattered the
mob, did I stick my own itching nose outside again.

The mosquito season in northwest Alaska is relatively
short—ten weeks at most, peaking in June or early July—but
it's savage by any standard. I've been pestered in tropical Asia,
mauled in the north woods of Maine, and chomped in the man-
grove swamps of Mexico. No bugs I ever encountered prepared
me for the mosquitoes of the Kobuk valley. At their worst,
there are untold millions per square mile, rising in whirling
vortices to engulf any unfortunate mammal. They can take a
pint of blood a *day* from a single moose, and stampede entire
herds of caribou into panicky, aimless gallops that biologists
call "aberrant running." Cows and calves get separated. Bands
are fragmented. Bulls flee until they're exhausted. And with
good reason. There are plenty of anecdotes suggesting that an
animal—or human, for that matter—caught in one of these bug
storms can be sucked dry.

Luckily, the worst infestations don't last for more than a
few days. Even the infamous early-season "Alaska state birds"
(averaging half an inch long) can't hack a moderate breeze.
They wither under bright sunlight. Too hot or too cold, too
much or too little rain, and they fade to reasonable numbers.
Bloodthirsty though it is, an arctic mosquito is a frail creature

that spends most of its six-week life hunkering under a leaf on the tundra, sipping plant nectar, waiting for the right feeding conditions. A still, humid, overcast evening is perfect. Then things can turn ugly in a hurry.

The upper Kobuk Eskimos know how to handle mosquitoes. As soon as the river is clear of ice, most Ambler people load up their plywood riverboats and head for the chilly, windswept coast to spend the summer, as they have for centuries. Of course, they're also fishing and hunting seals, but it's no coincidence that this annual migration sidesteps the worst of the bug season. The Inupiat don't complain about much, but they draw the line at mosquitoes.

If you stay upriver, good repellent and loose, layered clothing keep the blood loss down to acceptable levels. But that's not the real problem. On a bad day it's psychological warfare, airborne water torture. You're not safe outside, even in your own outhouse or walking to the post office. Up your nose, in your eyes and ears, there's never a moment's rest—thousands of hungry snouts constantly probing for a chink in your armor. The blur of perpetual assault brings on a creeping panic you have to ignore. And behind it all is that infernal whine.

There are people like Howie Kantner who show you it's all a state of mind. I remember watching him work one summer evening, wrapped in a horde of mosquitoes. I was slathered in repellent, waving a hand to keep them out of my face, and there was Howie, a *naluaqmiu* just like me, calmly measuring and sawing. Bare chested. No repellent, nothing. His back seemed to be covered with living gray fur. He didn't even seem to notice, unless one roosted on his lip or eyelid. Then he'd gently brush it away. "Oh, if you don't think about them, they won't bother you," he told me. "They're part of the country."

Howie's laissez-faire approach might explain why he's never weighed more than one hundred thirty pounds. He does have a point, though. If you spend summer in the arctic, mosquitoes are a simple fact of existence, an elemental phenomenon, like rain. You could ask, "Is it bugging out today?"

Yeah, a downpour. A bloody, bloodthirsty downpour.

The Only Game

❖

It's Friday night, and the Selawik Wolves are in town for high school basketball. The Ambler school gym, always busy, is packed—the four rows of bleachers filled, and restless kids jammed along the sidelines, maybe two hundred fifty people in all. This is one of only two home dates for the Grizzly girls, and though neither team has a winning record, the rivalry with Selawik, another Eskimo village eighty miles to the southwest, is enough to draw three-quarters of the village. In past years, I would have been coaching on the home bench, but tonight I'm just another spectator, sitting with my friends, enjoying the game.

This is not exactly all-star basketball. It's midway through the second quarter, and neither team has scored in several minutes. Ambler's top player, Jenny Williams, is shooting cold, and no one else seems able to even hit the rim. Passes sail out of bounds into the crowd, and one particularly enthusiastic shot by a Selawik girl slams the backboard so hard the rebound caroms over the half-court line. Groans and laughter ripple through the crowd. They're used to better basketball, as the two state championship banners on either side of the scoreboard suggest. Just three years earlier, the Ambler girls were the best small-school team in Alaska, known for their skill and discipline. But there hasn't even been a girls' varsity program for the past two seasons; there haven't been enough players in the tiny high school, whose total enrollment hovers around twenty-five.

This year, at last, there are just enough girls: five. Coach Autumn Rue couldn't send a sub into the game if she wanted to. If someone gets hurt or fouls out, the team will play on with four. Or three. She sits philosophically, cradling her young daughter on her lap. The Selawik Wolves, with two extra players, are in marginally better shape.

The crowd, in easygoing Inupiaq fashion, cheers for both teams. Most of the visitors are blood relatives, or the daughters of old friends. In the northwest arctic, a remote, roadless region the size of Maine, everyone seems to know one another, and the bonds of kinship are strong. When a Selawik girl finally makes a shot to end the scoring drought, everyone applauds as if the game were a cooperative effort. Tricia Douglas, an Ambler freshman, has the ball stolen from her. Instead of running downcourt to play defense she covers her mouth and giggles, and the crowd laughs along.

A few weeks ago it was another story. The Kiana Lynx, this year's top boys' team, were in town, and the two games with Ambler were more reflective of the passion the Inupiat have for basketball. Watching these young Eskimos dribble behind their backs and sink three-pointers, it's hard to believe that just fifteen years ago, there was no gym in Ambler, and few understood the game in more than a casual way.

Yet here, and in dozens of small villages across the state, basketball has risen out of nowhere to become not only the sport of choice, but a social phenomenon. From the rain forests of southeast Alaska to the windswept arctic coast, basketball is a central facet of contemporary Native culture, as much a part of life as hunting caribou, gathering spruce roots, or gillnetting salmon. Among many teenagers and young adults, fascination with the game seems to verge on obsession.

In Ambler, they're started young. Parents buy Michael Jordan paraphernalia and kid-sized hoops for children as young as five, and organized games for "Little Dribblers" fill the gym. Interscholastic competition starts in sixth grade with a school-sponsored program including uniforms, trophies, and air travel to tournaments across the region. High-school students buy hundred-dollar shoes and adorn lockers and notebooks with their uniform numbers.

The competition among the best is spirited, even downright fierce. Boys' and girls' teams called the Northern Lights, *Qaaviks* (Wolverines), and *Sussuanji* (Beluga Whales) play twenty-game schedules, all of which involve traveling hundreds of miles by chartered planes and landing on gravel runways at twenty-five below zero. At season's end, the regional champs fly six hundred miles to Anchorage for the Alaska 1A state tournament (limited to high schools with enrollment under fifty), and generally dominate the competition.

The expense to the Northwest Arctic Borough School District is enormous. Including coaches, uniforms, facilities, and travel, the dollar cost is measured in hundreds of thousands each year. And yet questions about the money are seldom raised; The People want basketball, and that's that.

This basketball mania doesn't stop at high school. Though few athletes are tall enough to play college ball, graduating seniors have been known to postpone, even forgo, job training or college in order to play "city league," a loose organization of teams that compete locally, and, sponsored by local businesses, travel to tournaments as far away as Nome and Fairbanks. I've had former students speak proudly of their "careers" playing for teams like Ron's Sales and Service or The *Napaaqtugmiut* (People of the Spruce Trees). Many of these city leaguers, approaching thirty, are unemployed, still living at home. They sleep all day and wait for the gym to open at 9 or 10 P.M., suspended, it seems, in a dream of fast breaks, layups, and applause from the crowd. Meanwhile, traditional Inupiaq skills—hunting, sewing skins, making birchbark baskets—quietly fade away.

I often muse over what's come to pass, and my own part in creating a world, three hundred miles off the nearest road, where basketball is king. The sport arrived in Ambler in 1979, the same year I did. The new high school, funded by state oil money, stood at the center of town, its gym larger than all the classrooms together. I coached successful teams, played city league, and taught fundamentals to my P.E. classes, both here and in Noatak, one hundred fifty miles to the northwest. Basketball was part of my job, and I believed in what I was doing.

Now I sit in the stands, watching the Grizzlies and Wolves battle it out. Ambler, though down to four players, is hanging on to a lead late in the fourth quarter. It looks as though the home team is going to win. The gym vibrates with excitement. Kids, adults, the old women in their bright calico parkas—everyone is cheering. I raise my hands and clap along.

Whistle for the Wind

❖

*A*arigaa, lots of berries!" Minnie Gray smiles.
Before her stretches the mountain-rimmed tundra of
the upper Redstone valley. With her oval-shaped
birchbark baskets in one hand, her *qalutak* in the
other, she waits for her friends Sarah Tickett and
Clara Lee to clamber up the steep bank from the
river. Though all three Eskimo women are around
seventy, their movements are spry, their faces lit by
girlish enthusiasm. They're dressed in women's work
clothes—knee-length calico pullovers, rubber boots,
scarves, and cotton work gloves. I've brought them

here in my jetboat, far back in the country, to a place they haven't seen in five decades. Minnie's grandson Eric, thirteen, has come too, wearing his UNLV basketball cap and shirt.

"Seeing this place again sure carry me back to my younger years," says Minnie. "I remember going up that mountain with my husband real easy, not stiff and slow like now. I was a young woman then, twenty years old." She reminisces about traveling up the Redstone in the late summer of 1944. All these years later she remembers the date, August 8. Clara recalls a day in 1931 when she and her family met some Unalakleet reindeer herders who'd come down Ivisaaq Pass, just north of here. Her voice trails off and she smiles, shrugging off the past. Before her lies the promise of an afternoon's work, and her childhood companions will share it. What could be better? The three women chatter in Inupiaq. Eric, who's grown up in Fairbanks and is visiting his *aana* for the summer, looks doubtfully up the valley, as if searching for the nearest Burger King.

Bent double, heads down, the women fan out, beating the low bushes with their *qalutaks* (resembling large, spoon-handled dippers, carved from spruce), knocking blueberries into their baskets, their movements steady and measured. Each works alone, intent as a foraging bear, as if survival hinged on filling her basket as quickly as possible.

And within the memory of these three women, it did. Fifty years ago, there were few cash jobs, no food stamps, no outboard motors or airplanes. Many upper Kobuk people still lived in scattered camps instead of villages, moving to places like this to gather momentary abundance. Wealth was a cache full of food, and when it was gone, times were hard. Though those days have passed—husbands dead, children grown, their grandchildren more at home in the village gym—Minnie, Sarah, and Clara work in the old way, each swing of the *qalutak* like the pendulum of an ancient clock, carrying them back to the world they knew.

I find a good patch and kneel, picking by hand. The berries are thick here in this little swale, plumped by recent rains. They clatter musically into my bucket as I push my fingers along, stripping each bush. These blueberries are different from the kind I remember in Maine years ago—more tart, ovoid rather than round, but just as fine in pancakes or a pie. Today I'm hoping for two gallons, which, like the ladies, I'll freeze in plastic bags for the coming winter. Every family in Ambler has one or two freezers packed with traditional foods, kept fresh through the warm summer months.

Before Ziploc bags and electricity, berries were stored in permafrost cold cellars, preserved in sugar and sourdock leaves, or in seal oil. In the brief picking season, mid-July through August, women and children would fill wooden barrels, birchbark baskets, or sealskin pokes with different varieties, each sought for its special flavor: creamy orange *akpik* (salmonberries); bright red, sour lingonberries; mealy, dark *paungat* (crowberries), low-growing bearberries, highbush cranberries, and more. Rich in vitamins, these and other plants—notably *masu* (Eskimo potato), willow greens *(sura)*, wild rhubarb, and sourdock—were an important part of the Inupiaq diet.

When I look up, Sarah is a quarter mile away, wielding her *qalutak* in surgical strokes, carving a swath through the bushes; a trail of full baskets tells me she's picked at least two gallons to my two quarts. Clara and Minnie are off to the left. Periodically, they straighten up and winnow out their berries, holding one basket overhead and pouring into another on the ground, letting the breeze carry away chaff. When the wind fades they whistle, asking it to help them in their work. Now and then they call to each other, their voices lilting in the valley's quiet.

Meanwhile, Eric is sitting on his duff, periodically rubbing insect repellent on himself. He picked for a while, and even tried his hand with the *qalutak*, but now he's lost interest. I suspect Minnie's disappointed, but other than scolding him when he walks where she's about to pick, she seems to accept that Eric's world isn't her own, and never will be.

As I work, I drift back to the story Minnie told me of her trip up the Redstone, ten years before I was born. She, her husband, and his parents lined their boats with harnessed dogs and pushpoles, forty tough miles upstream from the Kobuk. There were closer places to find berries and game, but her father-in-law was anxious, he said, to see this country one last time before he died. They made camp just below here, at Akillik, and planned to stay the summer. But on the evening of the fifth day, not far from camp, they spied three bears, not ordinary grizzlies, Minnie is careful to specify, but "shrew bears"—long-legged animals with the pointed snouts and vicious dispositions of their namesake. Minnie's father-in-law ordered them to pack up immediately; they would have left that night, had it not been so late. Looking upon such creatures, half beast, half spirit, was extreme bad luck, and the only way to avoid sickness or death was to flee at once. They headed down-river the next morning and never returned. Even today Minnie seems a bit anxious, and asks me to keep my rifle close by.

I could explain away shrew bears—no biologist or white hunter has ever seen one—but why not believe? In this wide country, there's room enough for all our dreams, even the small one that visits me now: on this tundra bank in the evening sun, Minnie, Sarah, and Clara are young again, their lives still ahead. They look to the sky and laugh together, whistling for the wind.

The Killing Field

Clarence and I crouch on the fall-bright tundra, rifles ready as the caribou move closer. Though this small group of bulls could choose other ways to go, they trot straight toward us, as if drawn. A maze of trails funneling out of the mountains to the north, grooved by centuries of passing, leads them to this place, this one bend of the river. Unless we jump up and wave our arms, they'll cross here.

As the caribou are led by the web of memory, so, it seems, are we. Behind us, overgrown by willow and alder, are circular depressions: ancient house pits, marking where people once sat watching as we do now. "Old-timers' place," Clarence calls it. Across the field, antlered skulls lie scattered, marking kills years or decades old. Sunk into the tundra are older bones, and the stone tools of those who left them. Past these the caribou trot, white manes shimmering.

"We'll just take one good one," breathes Clarence, and I can tell he wants me to shoot.

"Which?" I whisper. "The second? With the thick horns, or the first one?"

Clarence appraises. "Maybe that one," he says, pointing to the lead bull, a big-bodied animal with rack still in velvet.

Seventy yards away, they smell us. The bulls halt stiff-legged, staring. I chamber a round, rise, and fire. I know I've missed high. They mill around. I work in another shell, hold lower, and this time there's the *whump* of a hit. The lead bull stands for a second, head down, then his legs buckle. The others trot off, no more hurried than before. Five minutes later, we hear them splashing across the river.

Clarence wields his pocketknife, making a quick, speculative cut down the brisket. "Faat!" he murmurs with pleasure, drawing out the word as he always does. Trophy antlers are of no concern, and hides, in these days of down jackets and nylon, less important. But meat—good, fat meat—is still a measure of wealth.

We set to work, skinning and butchering, and the caribou flow south around us as if nothing had happened. A raven circles overhead, waiting its turn. Less than an hour later, we're headed toward home, the bow of our skiff heavy in the dusk, splashwater red at my feet. We've left the head leaning back on its great curve of antlers, throat open to the sky, another skull on the killing field.

Over the years, I've lost count—caribou, sheep, geese, moose, beaver, bear, a seemingly endless procession. Once I remembered each time: where I aimed, how it fell, what I felt. Each death was etched into memory, vivid and new, heavy with meaning.

I came to Alaska not much of a hunter, my experience limited to a few naive forays in the Maine woods and one whitetail buck I killed more by accident than skill. But I wanted to change that, to reinvent myself completely, to become someone who could skin a bear, wingshoot ptarmigan, read wolf tracks— all those things and more. It was no accident I ended up in an Eskimo village, among some of the last hunter-gatherers.

Not that I wanted to be a killer. What did I know about killing in those days? I just wanted to be around animals, to know their secrets, to move freely in their world. The best outdoorsmen I met here, men like Clarence, weren't just hunters. They were predators, pure and immaculate, tuned to every shift in the wind, to nuances of scent and sight I could only imagine. They weren't close to the natural world; they *were* the natural world. I wanted to know what they knew, and if that meant killing, so be it.

I got my wish. I found that I had some talent as a hunter— good eyes, quick reflexes, strength and patience. Going out on my own, following Inupiat hunters when they'd let me, copying the guide I worked for, I honed my skills. I learned where to look, how to stalk and shoot, how to take apart a moose with a jackknife. I found excuses to hunt, gave entire animals away so I could go back out.

But I never did learn how to kill, at least not the way Clarence does. There's no greater thrill for me than stalking a grizzly, no greater satisfaction than cutting into a caribou roast, and I'll admit that pulling a trigger and watching something fall stirs some deep, wild impulse I'd rather not face.

The ghosts, though, come back. One by one, over the years, they've piled up in my chest, some heavier than others. Some animals died almost willingly, giving themselves, it seemed, as the Inupiat once thought. Others refused, eyes rolling, roaring blood. Clarence might shake his head admiringly and say of a wolverine that went hard, "That bugger was tough," and leave it at that. I was never able to carry death's weight so easily, though I sometimes wished I could.

The small acts of reverence and propitiation, like *nigiluk*, cutting the throat so the soul might be reborn, offer small comfort. These gestures aren't mine, and they often seem lost in the roar of hundred-mile-an-hour snowmachines and twenty-round semiautomatic carbines.

This fall I saw thousands of caribou, but kept reaching for the camera instead of my rifle, putting off the inevitable. When I did shoot one, I gave most of it away. Finally, when the migration had passed, I ended up settling for a scrawny yearling, an animal Clarence would wrinkle his nose at. I needed the meat, and that's all there was.

Still I make my home here, in this most carnivorous of places, where carcasses lie heaped casually in every yard, meat racks bend under the weight of flesh, and drying hides shift like ghosts in the wind. This is what The People are, who they've always been—what I tried to be, and found I wasn't.

The Light Within

❖

It's too cold to walk slowly—fifty below zero and falling. Smoke from stovepipes curls upward, freezes, and sags back to earth. Drifting in a dense, crystalline pall that may last for weeks, the ice fog wraps the village in its own frozen breath. As I hurry up the dark street, parka hood drawn, I trail my own white plume.

The winter solstice passed three days ago. Somewhere around noon, dawn sagged into dusk, the edge of a night twenty hours long. Day after day, the sky remains pale and featureless; it's too cold to snow, too cold for wind to blow, too cold, it seems, for the sun to rise. If I could sleep through it like a grizzly and wake up in March, I would. I've heard newcomers claim that winter doesn't bother them. If they last three years (and most don't), they keep their claims to themselves.

In the upper Kobuk, the first snow flies around mid-September, and by the end of the month it feels like winter: ice floes grinding down the river, gray, stormy days, mornings of sharp cold. The intoxicating, eternal light of summer falls away with startling rapidity—five, seven, then eleven minutes a day. By early November the river is rock-hard, the sun barely clears the Waring Mountains, and we're still losing light. It doesn't matter that this winter is my fifteenth here. The change still catches me by surprise.

Now the serious cold begins. I wake up shivering one dark morning, and a flashlight on the outside thermometer shows thirty below zero. The water bucket in the corner has a skim of ice. From now until April, keeping warm is no longer a given. It takes constant, conscious effort. The woodstove roars at a full draft, roasting my back while my feet freeze. My Eskimo neighbors sum it up in a single exclamation—*Alappaa!* It's cold!

The worst cold snap usually comes in January. Temperatures fall to sixty, even seventy below, and stay there for weeks at a time. Although my log cabin is snug, frost coats the metal door hinges, builds up a half inch thick on windows, creeps up from the floor on inner walls. At these times, life curls inward like a sled dog in the snow, cradling its embers.

In deep cold, the laws of physics seem warped. Wood on

the chopping block shatters beneath the ax; steel snaps like plastic. If you want to start your snowmobile, you pour boiling water on the manifold to coax gasoline into vaporizing.

Getting dressed and undressed takes extra time. Like everyone else, I live in layers of acrylic fleece, goose down, and fur. Full winter gear—long johns, insulated pants, coveralls, parka, face mask, beaver cap and mitts, army surplus "bunny boots"—weighs up to twenty pounds. It's like walking around in football equipment padded with blankets.

But no matter how cold, the Ambler school doesn't close. There are church services and town meetings; the *Iviisaapaatmiut* hunt, cut wood, and travel between villages in all but the worst snaps, as they've always done. Whether it's their diet (rich in animal fat and protein), genetics, or sheer toughness, Eskimos shrug off weather that could kill an Outsider. Bareheaded teenagers walk to school in letter jackets and basketball shoes; hunters bear purple-black frostbite scars as badges of honor.

But it's easy enough to pull on another sweater, stuff another log in the stove. What gets me is the darkness. It gnaws from the inside, day after day, month after month, and no parka made can keep it out. Every November, with the fading of the sun, I slide into an aimless funk that rises and falls like the thermometer, but seldom gets above thirty below. On a bad day, getting out of a chair seems like work. Even caribou chili tastes like cardboard, and I catch myself sitting slackjawed through reruns of *Murder, She Wrote*.

People in the Lower 48 might call my affliction cabin fever, and scientists who study such things chatter about SAD— seasonal affective disorder. Around here, people simply call it what it is: The Darkness.

In the dim light and paralyzing cold, Ambler seems claustrophobic and dingy, my life here pointless. What possessed me to live in the arctic, anyway? I forget the day, just three months before, when I sat transfixed on the Hunt River tundra, watching thousands of caribou flow by, or the simple joy of watching my seventh-graders excited by an art project. Everything's suddenly gone sour. Play basketball with my friends? Nah. Take a snowmobile ride behind the Jade Mountains? Too far. Write? You gotta be kidding.

By late December I'm sleeping ten hours a day, downing two quarts of coffee to stay marginally functional, and wondering why, fifteen years ago, I didn't marry my college sweetheart, move to Tahiti, or become an accountant. The only consolation I have is the experience of fourteen arctic winters; I remind myself over and over that the fit will pass, that I'm not going crazy, and everyone else is fighting it, too.

But it's not my imagination. It does get worse every year. Howie Kantner, a white homesteader and trapper who lived out in the country for twenty years, once told me, "It's a cumulative effect. The winters pile up on top of each other, and finally the question is how many you can take." It's no coincidence that Howie and his wife, Irna, live in Hawaii now, growing coffee and macadamia nuts, wearing shorts every day. Dave and

Marcia opted for Arizona; Bob and Doreen headed for California. No one who spends twenty years in the arctic moves to Minnesota or Montana. Ever.

A March blizzard sweeps in. The snow stings like sand, piles in waist-high drifts. There's nothing to do but stay indoors and wait it out. After two days the wind fades into an afternoon of dreamlike calm and clarity. The Jade Mountains glow, and the promise of Spring is in the air. I turn to catch the sun on my face, to feel the light within. Although two months of snow and cold lie ahead, it's over. The Darkness has passed.

Outside the school, kids in T-shirts throw snowballs. Regina Randall, the school secretary, smiles as she walks by.

"Nice and warm, *ah?*"

"Yeah, sure is," I reply.

It's ten below zero.

The Trouble with Wood

❖

It's a clear morning in early April. Though the thermometer hovers just below zero, anyone who's seen a few arctic winters would recognize what the *Iviisaapaatmiut* call springtime. The sun's been up since 4 A.M., and the light is dazzling. You'd go snow-blind without dark glasses.

It's a perfect day for being out in the country—hunting caribou, skiing, visiting friends upriver. I have something more urgent in mind. My woodpile's getting low, and the snow, packed smooth by weeks of wind and cold, is perfect for hauling. Conditions like this won't last long; a sudden storm or a hot sun could turn the trails to mush overnight. Thirty sledloads of dry spruce, about eight cords, take me through a year. I reckon I have about half of what I need, and I've got two weeks before the snow collapses.

Thirty years ago, nearly everyone in Ambler heated with wood, cut by hand and hauled in a dogsled. Boys grew up at the chopping block, and cold nights echoed with the ring of axes. Now most homes have computerized oil heaters; fewer and fewer people rely on wood. Filling a drum at the village fuel project is much easier than messing with logs at thirty below, and doesn't cost any more. Fuel oil runs $3.40 a gallon; young men sell a six-log sledload of wood (roughly an eighth of a cord, cut with a chainsaw and hauled by snowmobile) for $50. Either way, it costs between one and two thousand a year to heat a one-room cabin like mine.

I'm one of the diehards who don't even own an oil stove. I'm not sure exactly why, but I actually enjoy the endless circle of chores—splitting two armloads a day, tending the stove at midnight, sweeping sawdust, tinkering with chainsaws, cleaning stovepipes. Maybe it's because the facts of wood are pure. They explain themselves.

Eskimos claim that the heat from a woodstove is different from an oil stove's, stronger somehow, more complete. I just know there's no better sound than the soft, hungry rush of a fire on a January night, no deeper satisfaction than knowing that you've pushed back the cold with your own hands.

Getting wood with a snowmobile is a technology all its own, something you learn as you go, and never quite get right—maybe because the whole notion of pulling thousand-pound loads through deep snow is crazy in the first place, especially with machines designed for play. The engineers who built these recreational toys would blanch if they knew.

The first thing you do to a new snowmobile is trash the stock hitch and weld up a heavy-duty replacement from angle iron and steel plate. You might modify the gearing, add wider skis, a few cleats. Then you need a flat freight sled, a tough, no-frills affair of plywood and reinforced lumber, with a bridle welded from steel pipe. It's strictly build-your-own. Throw in a chainsaw and some ratchet straps or rope, and you're ready to go make a fool of yourself—which everyone does getting wood, sooner or later.

I roar out of town in high spirits, my battered eight-foot sled flapping behind my equally worn Arctic Cat, my chainsaw freshly sharpened, my coveralls dry. I'm headed for the burn behind town, where a forest fire roared through twenty-five years ago, leaving endless acres of standing dead trees. The easy pickings are long gone. Most of the good stuff is eight, even ten miles out, in steep, willow-choked creekbeds. Making the main trails and keeping them open is, by necessity, a communal effort; the snow, up to six feet deep, has to be packed rock-hard.

Once you're out there, you branch off on your own. Everyone has his own preferred areas, his own style. I like to

snipe: find small pockets of wood close to town, in places others have overlooked or passed by. I develop my own little trail
system, work the area, and move on—one load here, three
there. The hillside I've found this time has at least eight sledloads of straight, dry trees, some more than a foot thick, and
only five miles from town. Of course, there's a catch. The only
way out is uphill for a quarter mile through bottomless drifts.
But I spent an hour the night before driving in circles, packing
things down, and I'm sure I can just pull up, whack down a few
trees, and drive home.

As I crest the ridge, I swerve to avoid a head-on with a cow
moose and calf who've decided the trail is theirs. I rev my
engine, clap my hands, and they finally move off. Business as
usual. Animal tracks crisscross these hills, and you often have
company. Coming home, I've seen where wolves and wolverines have walked in my trail just minutes before.

In less than an hour, I knock down six trees, cut them into
twelve-foot lengths, and ratchet down my first load. Things are
going so well that I decide to throw on an extra three logs. It's a
bit heavy, I know, but the trail should be good.

Not good enough. I make it a hundred yards before sinking
in a spray of snow. I grunt, tug, and cuss, but it's no use.
There's nothing to do but unload, muscle the sled forward a
few feet, load up, and try again. By the time I break free, my
clothes are soaked with sweat and melted snow. Another
fifty yards, and I'm stuck again. Then a third time. I should
throw off half my load, but I'm in the clutches of wood lust.

The devil on my right shoulder whispers, *Just a little farther. You're almost there.*

By the time I limp in, three hours after I set out, my coveralls are frozen into a cast, my fingers stiff as parsnips. On the way home, a ratchet strap broke and my carburetor got so iced up my machine wouldn't idle. I throw my load—three fewer logs than I started with—on the pile. My neighbor Lynn (who once used wood, but now heats with oil) saunters past, clean and dry.

"What happened?" he asks innocently. "Get stuck?"

"Not really," I mutter. I can tell by his eyes what he's up to.

"Say, Nick," he says, "isn't getting wood fun?"

That's just the problem. Somehow it is.

Mister Rue

❖

"Flying," says Dave Rue, "is ninety-nine percent boredom and one percent terror." He gives a wry laugh and shakes his head, as if wondering how he ended up here, a bush pilot in an Eskimo village. Six foot five and rough-hewn handsome, he looks the part, but his experience tells more. In twenty-three years of flying the northwest arctic, Dave's logged eighteen thousand hours of air time—eighteen thousand hours of bad runways, winter storms, and endless miles of sky. "Too many," he says.

While other plane jockeys have come and gone,

he's still here, one of the last of a breed: the owner of a tiny independent flying service, someone who knows the country well enough to look down in a whiteout, catch a glimpse of a treeline or a lake, and know where he is. In a place where everyone goes by first names, the older Eskimos still call him Mister Rue. At one time or another, he's flown search and rescue missions or emergency medical evacuations for almost every family in the upper Kobuk.

But it's not spectacular or heroic exploits that make a good pilot. It's the hundreds of flights that start out as routine and stay that way. Out here, people fly the way New Yorkers take the subway. The difference is every time you get in a plane—a small plane in the arctic—you're trusting the pilot with your life. The hills of Alaska are scattered with the wreckage of those who pushed their luck and found where it ended.

When I first got here fifteen years ago, I was impressed by flashier pilots, guys who swooped up canyons, set down on tiny patches of gravel, and sometimes came back with spruce boughs caught in their wheels. Dave seemed competent enough, but limited.

I saw the truth three years later, flying into Noorvik one January night for a basketball tournament. There was a fierce crosswind on the runway, gusts up to fifty knots. Our young pilot tried an approach, got knocked sideways, and pulled out. Then again. Other Cessnas were stacked up in the darkness, trying to get down. The pilot was talking to himself, obviously rattled. My kids were sick and scared. I was about to order him to Kotzebue when a calm voice came over the radio: "Two Six Hotel, coming in." Dave Rue slid in over the trees and landed his 207 as if this wind-blasted night were a summer day. Our young pilot did a double take, asked for advice, and followed him in. So did everyone else. Dave had made it look easy.

He came up as a teacher and started flying in 1971, figuring it was a good way to see the country. Five years later, Dave ended up buying Ambler Air Service, established by Dan Denslow, and found a new career.

It was still the bush pilot era. The region's ten villages had short, rough gravel landing fields, lit after dark by kerosene fire pots. Compasses and common sense were the only navigational aids beyond Kotzebue, the regional hub. "If the weather fell in behind you, you had to know the country," Dave says, with typical understatement. He's always been the sort who'd call a blown engine at five thousand feet a small problem.

Much of his work was in a Cessna 185, a single-engine workhorse that could lift just about anything you could cram inside. Landing on skis, floats, and wheels, he supplied homesteaders, dropped off surveyors and hunters. Ambler itself was served by only two scheduled mail planes a week. Ambler Air did the rest, flying charters between villages for church meetings, funerals, and basketball games.

At Shungnak one night, Dave made his first—and, so far, only—big mistake as a pilot. It was forty below, and he was in a hurry. Taking off without checking the field, he slammed a chunk of ice and ended up in the berm. No one was hurt, but a wingtip was crumpled, the prop bent. "I thought I was doing good," he recalls, "but I should have walked that runway."

Shungnak would prove to be an unlucky spot for Ambler Air. A few years later, Dave's engine failed on takeoff (he doubled back and made a clean landing), and then Dan Denslow, filling in one last time, crashed and burned there, killing six people.

"They say the ice fog got him, but I think it was probably mechanical," Dave murmurs. "I never have figured that one out." The unsaid words echo: *It could have been me.*

In the past fourteen years, there have been five fatal air service crashes in the northwest arctic—remarkably few, all considered. Three of these were collisions with mountains wrapped in snow or clouds. "Pilot error" is the terse, official explanation.

"Weather is what gets people most of the time," sighs Dave. "The more years you fly, the more you know what you can and can't do in certain kinds of weather. People do some stupid things."

The odds for safe flying keep rising. Though every village runway in the region is still gravel, they've been lengthened, and crosswind strips have been added, along with radio-controlled electric runway lights. Sophisticated navigational beacons reduce the guesswork in bad weather, and more air services are using twin-engine planes.

Traffic has increased dramatically, too. On some days, there are seven scheduled flights *a day* into Ambler, population three hundred fifty. The competition brought on by federal mail subsidies and airline deregulation has made small air services a marginal business, too small a pie for too many plates. Insurance premiums alone cost Ambler Air $40,000 a year.

The bush pilot era is history. Gone, too, are men like Bob Baker, Dan Denslow, and Archie Ferguson—men who put their lives into the country. In their places are new recruits, mostly earnest, highly qualified young men intent on piling up air time, hoping to fly commuter airlines or big jets. They work a few months at one of the larger air services in Kotzebue, then head south.

One of these days, Dave will be gone, too. "I'm pretty well burnt out," he says, and takes more time off each year. I ride with these new pilots who navigate the Kobuk with sectional charts in their laps, missing landmarks even the passengers know, and think of Mister Rue, his huge frame hunched over the controls, making it all look easy.

Coming Home

❖

I heave my pack from my shoulders. I'm home again.
When I last stood outside the cabin, it was early June,
and scraps of dirty snow clung to the woodpile; the
ground was sodden and gray. I've been gone just six
weeks, but in my absence, everything has changed.
Clumps of purple fireweed have overgrown my paths,
and mosquitoes buzz lazily in the still, bright afternoon. But the fireweed is already fading, and some of
the willows are tinged with yellow. Soon the first snows
will whisper over the tundra, and another season will
have passed. Summer has come and gone without me.

This August will be my fifteenth in the northwest arctic. The thought surprises me, even though I can account for the time; letters, notebooks, and photographs prove the passage of years, as do the broken sleds, the caribou horns piled outside my cabin. Still, I often feel like I fell asleep on a winter day and awoke to the cry of geese overhead. Fifteen years, one year, a thousand—the land remains the same. It's easy to forget that life is measured in heartbeats.

I pry the boards from the window, unlock the door. All is just as I left it—the battered old rocker with its bearskin pad, the table and chairs made from packing crates, the cast-iron woodstove. Everything seems familiar yet distant, blurred at the edges. I've just come back from Outside (which, to an Alaskan, means anywhere from Seattle to Timbuktu), and I know from experience that it will take a while before the crowds, the jets, and the rumble of traffic fade into the background. Every year I go for a few weeks, just to remind myself that there's a world beyond. If I stayed up here too long without a break, I might forget where I came from.

I remember heading Outside after spending my first six months in the bush, back in 1979. I was working for a hunting guide in those days, living in the same set of clothes for a week at a time, sleeping on the floor in the back of a trading post. Just in from skinning a moose at forty below, I'd jumped on a Twin Otter in Ambler and found myself in the Seattle airport six hours later, greasy and unshaven, my parka smeared with dried blood. Next to me in the terminal sat one of the most beautiful women I'd ever seen—a college student with long dark hair and blue eyes. I desperately wanted to talk to her, to explain where I'd been and what I'd seen. She studied her notes and refused to look my way. Slowly I became aware of a rancid odor curling around us, and then I realized it was me. At my feet, the frozen wolf head in my pack (a gift for a friend back home) was starting to leak. I might as well have been a wino from Mars. I sagged down into my chair. Travelers bustled past, well groomed and intent. Look at all the white people, I thought. I can't wait to get home.

All these years later, I look back and laugh. I'd been caught flat-footed by the shock, the sudden discovery that Outside, rather than the arctic, had become the strange, exotic place. Home had shifted three thousand miles north whether I liked it or not.

Now I sit in the old rocker in my cabin, wrapped in silence so full and rich that it seems a tangible thing, and feel my pulse slow to match my surroundings. This bouncing back and forth between cultures has become part of the lifestyle, something I've almost gotten used to. These days, when I step out of the Brooks Range and into a city, I treat the whole experience like an amusement park ride, jittery nerves and all. Caribou to street signs, mukluks to three-piece suits, the stillness of the tundra giving way to the rattle of jackhammers—the quick switch is sensory overload, like running through a crowd while looking through a kaleidoscope. I've learned not to take it all too seriously.

But the reverse journey is another story. Coming back to Ambler is something I do quietly, and I prefer to do it alone. The first few days, I find myself pausing often in my chores—splitting wood, hauling water, skidding my boat back into the river—just to watch and listen, to see again, with fresh eyes, this place I've come to call home. I sit on the roof, staring at the mountains: the jagged pyramids of the Jades; the Cosmos' rounded bulk; Old Man rising like a castle to the east. People stop and say hello, welcome me back, and I shake their hands, I'm happy to see them, but my eyes drift back to the far blue hills, and to the distance beyond. "Home," the sense of place that draws me back and haunts my dreams, isn't really here in the village. It's somewhere out there.

I haven't even finished unpacking before I'm loading up my aluminum jetboat—tent, sleeping bag, tarp, rifle, grub box, fishing pole, and enough gas to travel two hundred miles. I'd planned to stay in town a few more days, but my list of chores will have to wait. Gunning the eighty-five-horse outboard onto plane, then throttling back to cruising speed, I head up the Ambler River, then north onto the Redstone. Twenty miles. Thirty. The water is so clear I can see grayling darting away from the boat's shadow. Gravel on the river bottom blurs past, inches below my keel.

Hours later, in the pale silver light of late evening, I sit on a high bluff above the river. The mountains sweep up on either side, cradling the valley in their hands. Except for a cold wind falling from the north, the silence is absolute. Far across the tundra, a band of caribou trots past. I've come home, I whisper to them. They don't even glance my way. Home, I say to the mountains. There is no reply. I sit alone, staring north into the wind, waiting for the welcome that will never be offered, knowing that I haven't been missed.

Dollies

❖

Thigh-deep in the river, waders clamped to my legs, I brace against the current's cold rush. Though I'm sweating from the waist up, sun-scorched and hassled by mosquitoes, my toes are close to falling off. I've been wading and casting most of the day in this ice water runoff, with only a dozen grayling to show for my trouble.

I'll confess I've gotten spoiled. Some of those grayling I tossed back topped eighteen inches, blue-black males with huge dorsal fins, vibrant and cold in my hand. Once I would have been thrilled with so many good fish. Now I derrick them in and send them back without much thought. I'm looking past them, and past the mass of gray-green shapes I know to be chum salmon, intent on their spawning dance. Somewhere near the bottom of this pool, all but invisible, like ghosts of water and light, lie other fish: sea-run char of the genus *Salvelinus,* among the most beautiful and ephemeral fish in the world. I may be casting toward a few, or dozens, or none. There's no way to know.

At times like this, the end of a long day, shadows stretching across the river, I cast more out of habit than hope. I throw my line upstream, let the spoon sink, feel it tap the bottom as it tumbles and flutters, asking the river the same question over and over. The answer isn't important. What matters to me is the asking.

Against the far bank, there's a sunken tangle of roots, and the swirl of an eddy behind it. I've cast to the edge of this spot several times, deliberately fishing too shallow. I've already lost a half-dozen lures today, and don't feel like snagging one more. Still, I know that if there's a good fish in this pool, it should be there, against the bottom, just where the current breaks. I aim twenty feet above the pocket and work my spoon downstream, rod tip almost vertical, arms out, taking up slack.

Tap-tap. A pause, then *wham,* everything explodes. I lean back, reeling hard, then throw my rod low as line chatters out. The fish vaults from the river, cartwheels, and falls back with a wet crash. Before I can react, the fight changes directions twice, and I crank madly, trying to catch up. Another leap, and

❖

a long downstream surge; then it's a matter of steady pressure, pumping and reeling, letting line go and gathering it back, letting the rod wear down the fish. Finally it thrashes in shallow water, and I skid up a seven-pound female, fresh from the sea. In the pure evening light, she glistens like living steel.

They're singular fish, these char, so hard to pin down that even experienced fishermen often don't recognize what they've caught. Standing on the banks of some Brooks Range stream, they nod knowingly and talk of arctic char—a closely related, but entirely different species, *Salvelinus alpinus.* What lies before them is *Salvelinus malma*, commonly known as Dolly Varden.

Back in 1979, one month new to Alaska, I didn't even get the genus right. Out on a long trip through the Kobuk and Noatak headwaters, I wrote in my journal about the "salmon" I'd hooked. Years later, I was still mislabeling Dollies as arctic char, or sidestepping the issue by calling them "trouts," the way the Eskimos do.

Sometime in the mid-'80s, halfway up the Noatak, I met fisheries biologist Fred DeCicco, who knows more about char than most folks would ever want to. One of his duties back then was the arduous task of catching and tagging fish with rod and reel, the better to study their movements. Anyone smart enough to get paid for fishing, I figured, was worth a listen.

As Fred patiently explained, the distinctions between these two char, *alpinus* and *malma*, are clear. They have different numbers of gill rakers and pyloric caeca, and there are subtle differences in markings and shape—the thickness of the caudal peduncle, for example. If you don't know what a peduncle is, and couldn't care less, it's still easy to sort out the two species: river fish are Dolly Varden, lake fish are arctic char. This maxim holds true for arctic Alaska, though there are exceptions further south.

Issues of identity aside, there's plenty of room for head-scratching. Like salmon, most Dollies are anadromous; they eat and grow at sea, then return to spawn in natal freshwater streams—though, unlike most salmon, they go where they please in the meantime, sometimes roaming as far as Asia, often ascending rivers to overwinter far from their birthplace.

There are also isolated populations of year-round river residents, and dwarf forms in headwater streams. And two distinct forms of *Salvelinus malma*, northern and southern, overlap somewhere in southwestern Alaska. The northern Dollies are a race of mutants, bull-shouldered fish reaching twenty pounds, while the dainty southern variety seldom exceeds a third that weight.

To further complicate matters, *Salvelinus malma* are piscine chameleons. They suffer an inverted sea change at spawning time; their delicate silver-blue, pink-flecked markings intensify and darken, and the fish actually change shape, as some kinds of salmon do. Big males, especially, don't even look like the same species. Lean and humpbacked, sporting a hooked lower jaw, their bellies orange or flame red, lower fins white-edged, they have the brilliant, surreal look of plastic models painted by a color-blind taxidermist. By the next spring, the same fish are gaunt and faded, with oversized heads trailed by snake-like bodies. These spawners don't feed in fresh water, and live off fat reserves for as long as a year. Returning to sea, they'll slowly recover, transforming again into the sleek, silver creatures they were.

Though I've fished since I was four—rainbows in the Grand Canyon, smallmouths in Maine, corvina in the Sea of Cortez, coral trout off the Great Barrier Reef—I've never been so confounded or enthralled by a single species. A prime ten-pound Dolly is, to me, the most beautiful fish on earth. It's as if the mountains and sky, light and water of the Brooks Range were gathered through a living prism, distilled into an essence of place. When I hold one of these fish in my hands, I have the thing that I love before me, heavy and bright, iridescent with promise. I admire it for a moment, then give it back to the river.

Beautiful Meat

❖

We climb a tundra bank above the river, and Clarence grunts, "Bear." I follow his nod to not one bear, but four, less than two hundred yards away, against a tundra knoll. Heads down, they're feasting on blueberries, packing on winter fat. Since grizzlies are almost always loners, I know this must be a family—a sow with three grown cubs. I size things up. The wind is perfect, and there's enough cover for a stalk. I sprint back to the boat for camera gear, and sling my rifle just in case. Clarence shrugs and lights a Marlboro. He makes it clear he's staying right here.

Bending at the waist, I hustle forward, then drop down and crawl. When I ease over the rise, they're only forty yards away—the sow and one cub grazing, the other two sprawled out on the tundra. One has its front paws splayed in the air, twitching with bear dreams.

I brace my camera and burn through a roll of film. The light is perfect. Dwarf birch and willow flicker red and yellow, rattling in the wind. A raven's cry echoes from a distant line of spruce. I'm aware of all this, and of my luck in being here. These aren't the Denali Park or McNeil River bears you see posing on calendars and postcards. Bears around here are used to being hunted, and are almost impossible to approach. I'm sure my being this close depends on stealth rather than good-will, and, like most good things, it won't last long. Five minutes becomes ten. One more shot, I tell myself, and keep going.

All at once the cubs get agitated, standing like circus bears, backs straight. Then *woof,* the sow rears up. Maybe the wind swirled on me, or maybe the raven is to blame. I only know the bears are about to bolt—probably straight away, though there's no telling. I flatten out and snake backward, trying to duck behind cover.

But the sow drops down and lopes straight for me, huffing, her three two-hundred-pound teenagers in tow. It's not an all-out charge, but they're clearly locked on to my shape. Maybe they mistake me for a caribou. Maybe, too, this sow is that one bear in a hundred that doesn't avoid trouble. Either way, I'm on the hot seat. Any one of the cubs, each the size of an adult black bear, could break my neck with one swat. I back down the rise and out of sight, then sprint for the boat, waders flapping, camera clutched in one hand.

I know you're not supposed to run from bears, any more than you should run from a dog that's chasing you. I've stood my ground before. But it's only a couple hundred yards to safety. And hey, face it. This isn't one bear. It's a stampede.

I still have a good lead by the time I reach Clarence. "Here they come," I pant. "Let's get going." I'm keyed up, but clearheaded. There's no real danger, I know; the river is just another fifty yards. We can trot over, jump in the boat, and shove off. Clarence shakes his head, and stubs out his cigarette.

"Naah," he says. The bears are bounding straight toward us, mouths agape, shoulder humps rippling. Now they're too close to outrun. Clarence snaps back the bolt on his Ruger carbine, chambering a round. "I think I'll hunt one," he murmurs. "They look faat." He seems as calm as a woman picking over avocados in the supermarket, but I see him leaning forward, getting ready. I should have known better.

I'm trapped—not by the bears so much as by my friendship with Clarence. Moments like this define who he is, and all he is: an Inupiat hunter, part of a centuries-old tradition. Whenever we travel together, it's understood, of course, that we're hunting for whatever's in season—in other words, for whatever is "faat." Trying to talk him out of shooting makes as much sense as jumping between wolves and caribou, shouting for the madness to stop.

I knew all this from the start, but mistook Clarence's reluctance for lack of interest. He was, in easygoing Eskimo fashion, letting me go because I pushed ahead. Now it's his turn, and one man's photo opportunity is another's pot roast. I realize, with sinking heart, that I've unwittingly pimped this peaceful little family straight into Clarence's sights.

We're at the crest of a sandy knob, and the bears are thirty feet below us, moving slower now. We can't see them, but the sow's grunts and the crackle of willows tell us they're closing in. I know that if Clarence shoots, I have to join in. Clarence's rifle, though semiautomatic, is a real peashooter, with a bullet half the size of mine. No one in his right mind faces down a pissed-off bear with a .223. Except Clarence, maybe. He'll tell you a smaller bullet wastes less meat.

Suddenly the sow rears up before us. Her chest fills my scope. I have a flashing image of an old-time Inupiat hunter dashing in low to plant a bone-tipped spear. Instead, Clarence's carbine crashes, and I hear my own .243 erupt. The bear staggers, then topples backward, dead before she hits the ground. The cubs mill about. One bluffs a charge, and then they retreat, crashing downhill through the brush.

Clarence lowers his rifle. "She was pretty mad," he says. "Trying to get you for sure." He reassures me that the cubs are old enough to be on their own. There's no use arguing. I'm not too fond of either Clarence or myself just now.

The sow lies on her back, eyes glazing. We break her down, skinning quickly together, Clarence taking over on the butchering cuts. Working with a three-inch pocketknife, he severs joints and tendons with the effortless grace of a surgeon, rendering the carcass into neat, surprisingly bloodless packages: quarters, ribs, slabs of fat from the pillow on her rump. Even the spine is cut into chunks; paws are delicacies to be shared among village elders. "Beautiful meat," Clarence murmurs gently as he works. "Beautiful."

We leave only the badly worn hide, entrails, a few scraps. The head, as always, stays here. Clarence was careful, too, before he started skinning, to cut away "the worm," or cartilage beneath the tongue. Though he doesn't explain, I know these are precautions against the bear's spirit following us home. As we head up the windswept Kobuk, there's little to say. Somewhere behind us, there must be a place where all the ghosts wait. I can feel them gathering.

Remembering What They Knew

❖

A crowd gathers on the frozen Kobuk River—
women in calico parkas, men with their wolf-trimmed
jackets, restless children, elders—a quarter of Ambler's
three hundred fifty–odd residents standing together
on the ice in front of town. Though the November
morning is windswept and gray, ten below zero, faces
are expectant, the mood festive.

Yet there is no sign of a sled dog race or an
Eskimo football game. Instead, everyone is standing
around a fifty-yard-long V-shaped structure made of
whole spruce trees frozen into the ice. Only the

branched stumps protrude, as though dozens of trees were planted upside down into the river. At the apex of this funnel stands a canvas wall tent, and just beyond that tent door is a rectangular hole eight feet wide, a window into the dark water below. From this carefully chiseled opening juts a stout pole, angling downstream. Old men look down into the smooth current, nod and murmur to each other in Inupiaq. This is a *saputit*, a traditional fish trap, the first to be built on the upper Kobuk in over thirty years.

"Quiet!" a low, urgent command issues from the tent. Walter Gray, lying face-down over a smaller hole inside, has spotted a school of fish entering the trap. Any noise will turn them away. Mothers shush their children, and everyone falls silent, looking toward the tent.

"Quiet...quiet...quiet. Now!" People spring into motion, scrambling to help. Tony Foster hauls up on the pole, the handle of a cone-shaped net eight feet across and ten deep. As he lays the hooped frame flat on the ice, sealing the catch inside, a half-dozen women and men grab the mesh edges and gather the net upward, straining against a sudden weight. Then, moving as one, they spill the contents—a cascade of fish thrashing across the ice. These are almost all foot-long *kaalquk* (humpback whitefish), part of a huge annual run up the Kobuk. Children scramble after them, laughing and shouting, kicking them away from the hole.

Cries of *"Aarigaa!"* and *"Yaiiy!"* rise above the commotion as neighbors forget their differences and smile at each other, joined in the richness of the moment. These fish wriggling before them are the embodiment of what it means to be Inupiaq: hard work toward a common goal, reliance on traditional skills and the wisdom of elders, successful gathering from the land. It's a scene from an ancient past, when the survival of The People depended on such moments.

The women work swiftly, skewering the fish on green willows, fifteen to a stick, then laying them out in rows. Molly Penn, cigarette dangling, eyelashes frosted, grins at Mercy Cleveland and says, "*Alappaa*—It's cold!" and keeps working.

Through the day the rows grow as the net is raised—hundreds, thousands of *kaalqik* stretched across the ice in stiff bundles to be divided among the helpers. In the days to come, people will catch thousands more. Every family will have a share; some will be roasted or boiled fresh, others eaten as *coq*, sliced frozen and eaten raw, dipped in seal oil. "Fish caught this way taste different," Polly Downey tells me with a wide smile. "Better."

Village elder Truman Cleveland nods. The skills involved in building and using a *saputit*, passed down for generations, were in danger of being lost. With changes over the last few decades—snowmobiles taking the place of sled dogs, increased reliance on "store food" and a cash economy—people didn't need as many fish, and had learned to rely on modern gill nets, seines, and fishing rods. These methods were good, but what about the old Inupiaq way?

The Ambler elders, like Native elders across the state, had

witnessed the erosion of traditions over the past two generations. Their grandchildren, who seemed more interested in television and basketball than in sewing skins or hunting, couldn't even speak their Native tongue. Fifty years ago, growing up in isolated camps, there had been few distractions. Children learned everyday skills by watching their parents, and there had been no question that they would. Now, kung fu videos, rap music, and the village gym compete for attention. Bootleg alcohol and drugs make matters worse. What would these children teach their own?

The elders, normally content to tell stories on Inupiaq Day, decided to take matters into their own hands. For years there had been talk of making a fish trap, but no one had ventured beyond words. True, this was work for younger people, but it was clear that if there were to be a *saputit* ever again, it would be up to the ones who wanted it most.

Truman spread the word the usual way: over the village CB radio network. The lengthy announcement ended in a call for volunteers—young men with snowmobiles and chainsaws to gather trees, others to hack holes in the foot-thick ice. In an Eskimo village, a request for help, whether to haul a boat or dig a grave, seldom goes unanswered. An entire crew showed up, more or less at the appointed time.

Merrill Morena, who had built *saputit* as a young man, lent his skill, and other men added what they could. There were details to recall, all vital to success. The trap couldn't be put just anywhere; the apex must be exactly in the center of the current, or the fish would turn back, and the water had to be the right depth. The river bottom should be clean, light-colored gravel, so spotters could see fish entering the net. Then there were minor points, refined over the centuries but now blurred from disuse—the angle and dimensions of the *saputit* for a given channel, the size of trees, the depth of the net (which had to be built from scratch, from plans that had never been written down). The elders gave directions and conversed; the younger men made up for their lack of experience with enthusiasm; the women, as always, cooked for the workers and did their part.

And now, on this windswept November day, The People join on the frozen river. Together they bring up fish in the old way, thousands heaped like coins on the ice, more than enough for everyone. Caught in a sudden burst of sun, the *Iviisaapaatmiut*, The People of the Redstone, leave the world of basketball and television behind, and remember what they had almost forgotten.

The Hardest Season

❖

Steve and I lean against our snowmachines, looking out across the rolling, open country along the shoulder of the Cosmos Hills. It's one of those crystalline arctic spring afternoons, so quiet you can hear the creak and rustle of winter collapsing. Even strained through dark glasses, the glare hammers my eyes. Tundra stretches east, broken by thin lines of spruce, and blue-shadowed mountains drift beyond. The cry of a distant raven cuts the silence.

"They're out there somewhere," Steve murmurs. In every direction the snow is torn and trampled, pawed down to bare ground in places. Trails grooved two feet deep lead toward Ingichuk Pass. We can see at a glance that many of the hoofprints are fresh, the edges not yet blurred by melt or sifting snow.

The western arctic caribou herd, half a million strong, are marching toward their calving grounds in the Utukok Hills, just inland from Point Lay. After wintering on the windswept tundra between the Kobuk and the Yukon, they face an imposing journey, up to three hundred miles through the jagged sprawl of the Brooks Range. Late April and May in the arctic means breakup: a time of melting snow, rotting ice, and bottomless trail. To traditional Inupiat, trapped by the thaw in their camps, this was a season of hardship, perhaps starvation. Even bull moose sometimes give up and die in spring slush. Yet the caribou pour northward at breakup, shrugging off the impossibility of their going.

Many won't make it. The weak starve or fall to disease; others drown in ice-choked rivers, or stumble and break legs. Native hunters on snowmobiles roar out to fill empty meat caches, greeting passing bands with volleys of gunfire. And wolves, the caribou's ancient companions, are never far away. Tufts of hair and splintered bones lie scattered across the tundra, marking kills.

But the caribou press on, straggling north in long files, heads down. The cows, especially, sense the urgency. Most are pregnant, soon to give birth, and their young stand a far better chance if born on the calving grounds. The huge, loose herd that forms there, hundreds of thousands of caribou gathered like individual cells of a huge single organism, offers insulation from predators as well as insects. There can only be so many wolves or mosquitoes per square mile. By bunching together, the caribou improve their odds.

Steve and I crest a ridge and there, as far as we can see, are caribou: bands of ten to fifty, heads down, grazing. A few animals spot us, but we're a quarter mile away, too far to cause alarm. We leave our machines and creep forward, cameras ready, intent on getting close.

"Stay low," I whisper. There's not much cover, but we follow a line of scrub willow to within two hundred yards, then inch closer, crouching in the snow.

These aren't the same animals that swept south last fall, white manes gleaming, clashing horns. If the southward migration of the caribou can be compared to the advance of an army, the northward return has the aspect of retreat, of beaten survivors straggling back home. Their coats are sun-bleached, dingy, shedding in clumps. The spectacular curving antlers of the big bulls have long since been shed; their ribs show through. Some have lost fifty pounds, a seventh of their prime weight.

First there was the frenzy of the October rut, when the bulls threw all their energy into fighting and mating, exhausting fat reserves just as winter set in. Then came seven months of storms and deep cold, of pawing through the snow for mouthfuls of frozen moss. Now they face the hardest season of all.

Not all the caribou's adversaries are obvious. Beneath the shabby coats, just under the hide, are hundreds of inch-wide festering cysts, each cradling a white segmented grub—the larva of the warble fly, a parasite so fierce it seems predatory. Laid on the leg hair during summer, the larvae penetrate the hide and migrate to the animal's back. They spend the winter burrowed into their host, feeding steadily, draining away energy. Now that spring is here, the grubs gnaw through the hide and drop onto the tundra, pupate until summer, and sprout wings to plague the caribou anew. It's no wonder that a single warble fly can stampede an entire band into a thirty-mile gallop—something no wolf pack could ever do.

Then there are botfly larvae, clustered at the back of the throat in clotted masses that interfere with breathing. These, too, are nearing maturity, at a time when the caribou have no strength to spare.

Despite—or perhaps because of—constant hardship, the caribou prosper. There are thirteen separate Alaskan herds, each defined by its own ancestral calving grounds. No matter how far they travel, caribou return to that one area each spring, drawn by some inner music. In a life of wandering, the memory of birth offers the only certain destination.

The western arctic herd is by far the largest in the state, and it's still growing at a rate of 12 to 15 percent each year. No one knows what triggered the explosion, or where it will stop. Eighty years ago, caribou were scarce in the Kobuk and Noatak valleys; as recently as fifteen years ago, the hunting limit was two a season. Now it's five a day, year-round, reflecting a tidal bounty that may recede as quickly as it came.

I work quietly, edging closer a few feet at a time, pausing now and then to change camera lenses. As we move inside a hundred yards, a few cows show signs of agitation—staring stiff-legged, then turning heads, scanning for other threats. Gradually they relax, go back to pawing and feeding. We slide forward again, and, without warning, one animal rears up and spy-hops on her hind legs, an alarm that surges like a wave through the herd. Dozens of animals join the stampede. A muffled thunder rises from behind the ridge, and suddenly we find ourselves on the edge of hundreds of caribou we hadn't seen, galloping past in a snow-clouded blur, cows, bulls, and yearlings running heads out, nostrils flared. A thousand, I count to myself. Two thousand. More.

"Jesus," says Steve, more to himself than to me.

It's hard to remember that this is a tiny fraction of the western arctic herd, and that this pass is only one of many. On our small stage, in this instant, the caribou seem endless.

The band slows and gathers itself, forgetting us and their momentary panic. As we watch, they trot uphill toward Ingichuk Pass, thousands moving as one, heading north, hearing only the song that leads them home.

Dumb Head

❖

The whole thing started innocently enough. My canvas wall tent was leaking, and needed a coat of sealer. I'd pitched it a few weeks before, forty miles out, figuring to leave it up through September. Lashed to a spruce pole frame and heated with a woodstove, the seven-by-nine was nearly snug as a cabin...except for the leaks. The fall weather had been miserable—sheets of rain mixed with wet snow, and the drips were getting old.

Simple enough to fix that. On my next trip down-river, I lugged along a gallon of sealer, and the next morning fired up the stove and started sloshing the stuff on. Twenty minutes tops, I figured. As soon as I was done, I'd head out for the day with my camera gear and let everything dry. Just this last section around the stovepipe.

Then, without warning, the tent—*the whole damn tent with all my gear inside*—was blazing, as if someone had poured gas down the ridgepole and tossed a match. I glanced at the river, ten steps away, and knew there wasn't time for water. The tent was already lost. *But my gear!* Cameras, rifle, sleeping bag, pack, grub box, spotting scope—it was all in there, wrapped in gouts of flame and black smoke. I sucked in a deep breath, dove through the open flap, grabbed what I could, and heaved it out. Then I was rolling in the snow, coughing, jacket and gloves smoking.

Inside of two minutes, there was only a frame, a stove, the brass grommets at the corners, and a rectangle of smoldering ground. The tent had vaporized, as if a magician had waved his wand. As it all sunk in, I did the only thing I could have: leaned back and laughed like the fool I'd been. A few drops of sealer, obviously a good substitute for rocket fuel, had dribbled down the stovepipe and flashed back up. I'd incinerated a few odds and ends, and scorched holes in my clothes, but I knew I'd been let off with a slap.

I grew up steeped in the myth of the early American frontiersman, guys like the Deerslayer, Davy Crockett, and Daniel Boone. Like most kids, I believed that a real man never screwed up in the woods, not ever. And, after fifteen years traveling the

Brooks Range, most people would say I know my way around. I shoot my own meat, haul my own wood, read animal trails, and so on.

But more often than I'd care to admit, I make boneheaded mistakes out in the country, from minor to life-threatening. I'm just as capable as ever of sinking a sled in overflow, missing a caribou at fifty yards, or stepping backward off a cliff. Experience is no guarantee against stupidity. It just cuts the lag time in figuring what you should have done.

At least I'm not alone. Even my Eskimo friend Clarence Wood, who's lived here all his life, isn't beyond slamming his boat into a gravel bar he knew was there, or dropping a snow-machine through the ice...not to mention the holes *he* burned in my tent last spring when he borrowed it. I'd given him hell, so I knew he wasn't going to let me forget that I'd finished the job. He'd throw back his head and laugh, then tap a finger to his temple. "Dumb head, *ah?*"

Sure, everyone makes mistakes, but some folks seem to have a natural talent. The undisputed champ around here is Olaf Allison, a teacher from Kiana. Over the past fifteen years, his improbable shenanigans have become legendary up and down the Kobuk, told and retold, embellished here and there, even though the truth is good enough. When someone talks about "pulling an Olaf," you know it was no ordinary screwup.

For starters, there's the time Olaf, out spring hunting, pulled a "dead" beaver into his boat and laid it by his feet. A few minutes later, it came to, hissing and snapping. A wounded beaver is nothing to fool with, and you can't completely blame Olaf for getting excited. But shooting downward *inside* the boat was, at best, a poor choice. Fired point blank, the bullet had two options: pass through the bottom (as it should have) or ricochet back where it came. It chose option two, and Olie just missed getting a bad haircut.

Olaf used to live up in Shungnak, on the edge of a fifty-foot bluff, more of a cliff, really. One fateful day he fired up his snowmachine, a big Swedish clunker called an Ockelbo, notable for being one of the first machines to have a reverse gear. Olie, careless or in a hurry, gunned the engine and rode grandly off the bluff, backward and straight down. It's said that God watches over madmen and children. Olaf, being a little of both, fell clear, hit some soft snow, and walked away...only to repeat the stunt a few weeks later on the same machine, this time in forward, with a thirteen-inch color TV in his lap. Seems the TV jammed the throttle wide open when he turned the handlebars. Though the set was never quite the same, Olaf, trading in another of his nine lives, lived to create his masterpiece: the Maniilaq River Boat Bonfire.

Olie was headed upstream alone, so no one can be sure of what really happened. The story you hear most often goes like this: he somehow got knocked out of his boat by a sweeper—a tree hanging low over the water, blocking twenty feet of a channel maybe fifty yards wide. This was no mean feat by itself, but Olaf was just getting started. He dragged himself back in the boat and gunned it for the nearest gravel bar, intent on building a fire. Beaching near a pile of driftwood, he dragged one of his plastic gas cans there, sloshed a bunch on the brushpile, and threw on a match. That's when he discovered that the can had leaked all the way over and left a pool of gas in the boat for good measure. Just like in the comics, the flame followed the gas trail back to the boat, and *whump*. The rest is history.

I'd laugh at Olaf harder, but next time I know it could be me, or any of us. I'll bet Davy Crockett pulled a few "dumb heads" too. He just lucked out. No one was looking.

One Leaf

❖

It's not much—a single willow leaf, yellow, curled at the edges. At first I thought it was a candy wrapper caught in a branch. The early August sun rests warm on my back as I work outside the cabin, and white-crowned sparrows flicker through the trees. Forty miles to the east, a thunderhead billows against the dream-washed bulk of Old Man Mountain. But the leaf knows the truth, and so do I. Summer's over.

It's hard to believe, looking at this vibrant green landscape, that it will burn bright, fade, and drift into snow, all in just three weeks. Arctic seasons blow open and shut like doors in the wind; the change is startling, something I've never gotten used to. There's often a single week you can point to, sometimes a day, that marks an edge.

The calendar isn't much help. While the solstices do mark the height of summer and the depth of winter—the arctic circle being the line where, on the longest day, the sun never sets and, on the shortest, never rises—the equinoxes seem skewed. The official first day of spring can mean forty below zero and snow to the eaves. On the autumnal equinox in September, fall, instead of beginning, is ending—thickening ice, snow, nights of sharp cold.

Still, the old joke about the two arctic seasons, winter and fall, is off base. Ambler may be among Alaska's cold spots (four winters ago, we held between forty and seventy below zero for twenty-one days straight), but you'd never guess that from the almost tropical intensity of a midsummer day. From late May to early August, the sun hardly sets, carving an elliptical path above the horizon, hammering down from all points of the compass. Frost can hit on the Fourth of July—this is, after all, the arctic—but eighty degrees on a cloudless day isn't unusual, and nineties aren't out of the question. That makes for an annual temperature swing of one hundred fifty degrees, in as little as four months.

Add to that the manic extremes of light: near-total darkness to unending day in just six months, then back again. If there's a way to avoid this seasonal whiplash, it's news to me. Late this May, I woke from a nap at 9 P.M., yanked on my school clothes, and hustled for the door, convinced it was morning and I'd overslept.

I'm not alone, either. The whole village goes haywire in late spring. Friends drop in to visit at midnight; second-graders stagger into school bleary-eyed, bragging they "never sleep yet." You can't blame me, a few years ago, for shooting my alarm clock full of holes.

Eskimos, as you'd expect, start melting when the mercury hits seventy-five. "*Adii*, too hot," elders complain, and there's still snow on the ground. As soon as school's out and the ice breaks up, half the village packs up and boats downriver two hundred miles to Kotzebue's windswept coast, where people find seasonal work as well as a break from the heat. Those who stay upriver sweat in houses built for winter.

After the frantic bustle of spring, summer life in Ambler turns languid. There are no caribou to hunt, the geese have passed, and it's too early to set salmon nets. Now that school's done, few people are out and about before noon. Most people "get backwards," keeping odd hours through the cool, bright evenings, sleeping into the afternoon. High schoolers play basketball outside at 2 A.M.; the women pick berries; men set out at midnight to hook sheefish. The only ones exerting much energy are the kids. Sun-browned and wearing shorts, they ride bikes, play "Lapp game" (an odd, scoreless, winnerless variant of baseball), and cool off in the Kobuk's bone-chilling waters.

But from the heady week of solstice, when the sun never sets, the light keeps falling away. At first it's just a minute a day, but the pace quickens, the midnight twilights deepen. Winter's coming, though the sun burns down and fireweed blooms.

By mid-August, night is dark enough for stars, and the morning tundra creaks with frost. "Falltime," people say. "Time to get busy." The men sight in their rifles, and search for a fat bear or moose. The women fish in earnest, endless cycles of checking net, cutting, and drying. It's time, too, to gather cranberries, wild rhubarb, and *masu*, Eskimo potato. In the still, luminous days between the first cold rains, the cry of wild geese echoes down the sky.

At last, like a floodgate opening, the caribou pour south, endless white-maned waves shimmering across the tundra, the antlers of the herd bulls trailing shreds of velvet. Hunters wait at the river crossings or on the rolling, open hills behind town. The distant crackle of gunfire carries back on the wind, and piles of carcasses grow by the meat racks.

Meanwhile, everyone's back from Kotzebue. School's started. Though these first few weeks are the best of the year, everyone fresh and eager, I can't help turning to the window, staring out across the flats, where each leaf blazes red and gold. To the west, snow squalls pile against the Jades, then clear in brilliant rifts of blue.

I rush home most afternoons, throw my gear together, and head out on the river. If anyone asks why, I don't have a good reason. I already have my fall meat and a freezer full of fish. There are bills to pay, papers to grade, a sled to repair, but, just now, those things aren't important. Sometimes I run downstream a few miles and sit on a high bank, listening to the river, facing into the sun. I know it's only winter coming, but I find myself saying good-bye to all the bright things of this world, to the time that, just a month ago, seemed to last forever.

Leaves fade and fall; one day the caribou are gone, quick as they'd come. The *Iviisaapaatmiut* heave their boats ashore and let them sleep. As wind eddies west, then north, slush whispers downstream in growing clumps. Shelf ice reaches out into the current, sealing away the water into hard silence, more each day as the river cools, until, sometime in October, only a few steaming runs remain. I watch them close one by one, and feel myself settling with the land, drifting down into the cold, white dream. Far to the south, the sun leans against the Waring Mountains. I open my hand and let it go.

I Pick Your Name

❖

It's Christmas Eve in Ambler, thirty below zero. Bundled against the cold, I hurry up the trail toward the Friends Church. Tonight is the community Christmas program, one of the year's big events in any Eskimo village. As usual, I waited until the last minute to wrap presents, and now I'm late. A snowmobile rattles past, the sled basket filled with gifts and children. Everyone waves, and I answer.

This will be the first Christmas in the new church. A sleek one-story building on the edge of town, it boasts a computerized oil heater, painted

141

drywall, and a linoleum floor—a far cry from the drafty old log
church by the river, with its oil-drum woodstove and plywood
walls. Even though the average Sunday attendance is under
fifty, the new church can hold several hundred people; it was
built with gatherings like Christmas in mind.

I swing open the door from the frost-filled *kanisak* (storm
shed) and step into the bright, communal warmth of an Inupiaq
Christmas. Nearly everyone in Ambler has come, not only to
watch the program but to participate, and to give gifts, and
watch everyone else receive theirs. I think back to the
Christmases I knew in Maine; how most of the decorating, the
giving, and the celebrating was turned inward, shared only with
close family and friends. Churchgoing and social gatherings,
pleasant enough, were token public appearances.

Here, it's different. Most people in Ambler are related
somehow, and everyone knows each other. In that sense the
circle of Christmas is the same as the one I knew, only larger.
But the Inupiaq love of shared celebration transcends the
bonds of kinship. Here, every part of Christmas is public, down
to the last scrap of tinsel—a church service every day for a
week, a program at the Ambler school (complete with a visit
from Santa Claus), a village-wide feast on Christmas Day, a
community gift exchange, and the main pageant tonight.
Almost every gift between three hundred fifty–odd people,
from a new rifle down to the last pair of work gloves, is given at
the church, with the name tag read aloud.

The church is ablaze with decorations: strings of flashing

lights, garlands and bells of multicolored tinsel, a ceiling-high tree in full regalia, and an enormous Nativity mural on the front wall. Heaped around the tree chest-high, a mountain of gifts threatens to spill across the stage and into the pews, cardboard boxes and plastic sacks full, some wrapped, some straight from the store, price tags and all. The more extravagant items, including a matching washer and dryer, a dogsled, and a recliner, are displayed for all to see. I hand my bag of presents to Stan Johnson, and he adds them to the pile.

I slide into the wooden pew next to my friends Lynn and Carol. The program started half an hour ago, but I haven't missed much. Just handing out presents takes a couple of hours, and before that come dozens of songs, speeches, and "pieces"— short recitations of Christmas verse. Anyone who wants a piece can get one at the pastor's cabin. In fact, all who want to sing, give a skit, or speak are welcome to take a turn, whether or not they've rehearsed. If you sing off-key or forget lines, everyone claps just the same. Quality isn't important; taking part is what matters.

Miles Cleveland, Sr., presides, handing over the microphone as people take their turn on stage. Christina Cleveland and Tricia Douglas sing "Away in a Manger" in Inupiaq:

Niginavingmii sinigviiksrailaamii...

Their angelic voices rise over the constant undercurrent of murmured conversations, toddlers playing in the aisles, latecomers arriving. But the generous applause shows that people were listening.

"Thank you, ladies," says Miles, and consults his notes. "Lena and Eva." The two young girls have a piece to say together. Everyone leans forward as Lena, long dark hair shining, begins:

Jesus came to Earth to be

Savior of someone like me.

She passes the mike to Eva, who rolls her eyes to the ceiling, lips tracing words, then recites with obvious relief:

Came to Earth long ago

Came the love of God to show.

"Thank you, girls," says Miles, and the program rolls on— a country trio led by Tony Foster playing "Silent Night"; Steve Cathers, the Ambler school principal, singing a traditional Spanish carol. Elder Tommy Douglas tells stories of Christmases fifty years past: "We never had much stuff to give each other, not like now," he says, gesturing at the heaped gifts. "But we always remember Jesus and we're thankful."

Among the many pieces and songs, Lynn, Carol, and I take our turn, singing "Hail to the Newborn King." As I look out at the faces of friends and neighbors, people I've known for years, my jitters vanish. It's as if I'm singing to my family far away.

Sometime after 9 P.M., Miles runs out of scheduled acts. "Does anyone else want to sing or say something?" he implores, and the show goes on for another half hour.

Only when no one will come forward does the gift exchange begin. Arthur Douglas, Sr., in charge of the tree as always, calls for volunteers from the audience—people to read tags aloud, others to carry gifts. Besides the hundreds of presents between friends and family, everyone has drawn a name for a gift exchange. On each of these tags is written I PICK YOUR NAME. Mayor Cornelius Douglas, Walter Gray, and Frank Johnson take turns reading:

To Aana Edna Greist from Elwood Brown, Sr.,
I Pick Your Name....
To Nelson Greist, Sr., from Jim Wilson,
I Pick Your Name....

And so it continues for two more hours, each present handed out individually. Large gifts warrant applause, and so do handmade mukluks and beaver-skin caps. The announcers grow hoarse; people smile, converse, and unwrap gifts; sleepy children whimper. Slowly the pile around the tree dwindles, until only the bags of Christmas candy and popcorn remain, one for every person. It's nearly midnight, and the program started at six.

"I guess that's all for this year," says Miles. "Merry Christmas!" People gather boxes and bags, pull on parkas, and trail out into the night, still reluctant to go. Walking home, I think of my parents five thousand miles away. I only wish they could have heard us sing together, missed notes and all.

Wolves Are Listening

❖

The wolves must have seen me first. In the slanted sunlight of late evening, they couldn't miss a bright orange tent, a snowmachine, and a man on the valley floor. I looked up, wondering what had spooked the sheep, and saw them: a trotting black wolf, then a gray, silhouetted against the snow. As I swung my spotting scope around, I found ten others, strung out along the ridge. One limped heavily, a paw curled to its chest. They worked across the snowfield, down into a draw, and out of sight.

I went back to camp chores, feeling lucky. Even

though local wolf populations are close to an all-time high, riding the crest of a caribou boom, planning to see some on a given day is like going out on a Friday night expecting to fall in love. The best you can do is to hang around likely places, keep your eyes open, and try not to be disappointed.

Even far back in the western Brooks, most packs have learned the hard way about us. The limping wolf might well have lost his toes in a No. 4 Newhouse set by a *Nunamiut* trapper. Illegal airplane hunters, too, range across this country, sometimes wiping out entire packs. Any wolf that isn't cautious around humans is pushing its luck.

But these wolves didn't run, though they paused and stared toward me. Maybe there was something about the way I stood or even what I thought that reassured them. If wolves are experts at anything, it's reading intentions.

I cooked dinner and watched the upper Noatak slide into the twilight that, in late April, passes for night. As I sat alone, a chorus of howls rose from the mountain behind me, then faded into the wind.

I awoke the next morning to more howls, much closer now. I could hear the aspiration at the end of each wavering call. Stumbling from the tent into the bright blue day, I scanned the ridge behind me. Nothing. I set up the spotting scope and went to work. There, a head on the skyline, five hundred yards above me in the rocks. I was being watched, and no doubt discussed.

I howled back. A second head, this one black, popped up,

peering down in apparent incredulity. I made a mental note to work on my accent.

Scanning with the scope, I found other wolves as they crested the ridge. They apparently wanted to move downhill, on a course that would take them right through camp. Either I'd set up on their usual trail or they'd come because I was here.

Slowly, one at a time, in almost imperceptible movements, they made their way down, one here, two there. If I sat and watched, they moved little or not at all, feigning indifference, plopping down and curling up as if for a quick nap. When I ducked into the tent and checked five minutes later, they'd shifted closer.

After a half hour of this, I was getting edgy. I'd been close to wolves before, but the contact was fleeting, accidental—usually little more than an instant of startled recognition and a flash of fur. This was different. They'd seen me, and were making a deliberate approach. Nothing in my experience told me I was in danger. But how many people have sat calmly, alone, as a dozen wolves worked their way into camp?

All the warnings I'd heard from older Eskimos swirled back. Clarence, the master wolf hunter, had admonished me to be careful around large packs. He told me how to meet them if they came into camp: don't shoot, wave, or shout, just stand outside the tent facing them, showing calm resolve—the same message, I suppose, a surrounded moose hopes to send.

"Wolf can get me anytime, real easy," Clarence had said. "If they want to, well, nothing I can do." When I replied that I wasn't afraid of wolves and tried to counter with my white-guy feel-good-about-wolves-they-are-our-brothers statistics, Clarence grew suddenly irritated. "Quiet! Wolves are listening right now!" His tone of voice was the same as when he'd warned me I'd unknowingly crossed some dangerous ice.

It took almost an hour for the first two grays to reach the bottom. They dropped into the brush and disappeared a hundred yards away, still angling toward me. I suppose I should have waited. But what if I just sat here and they passed just on the other side of that knoll? I shouldered my camera tripod and hustled to intercept them.

From the crest I spotted one gray loping off, pausing to look back. The other seemed to have evaporated. This was wolf behavior I understood. I watched and waited, was about to give up, when I spotted the other lying behind a clump of willow, close enough to make me start. But though I was in plain sight a few dozen yards away, the young male ignored me, gazing off down the slope. When I moved closer, he rose, stretched, and regarded me with casual interest. There you are, he seemed to say. So what? When I inched closer, he moved off an equal distance, a long stone's throw away. After a few minutes of this interspecies two-step, he trotted off, apparently bored by my company.

Suddenly he stopped, intent on something before him. He gathered himself, pounced, and came up with an ordinary-looking willow stick. Shaking his head like an overgrown puppy, he paraded off with his prize.

When I looked back up the hill, the rest of the pack was moving off, retreating over the top or circling west on the ridge. The two grays, I guessed, had been scouts, and my approach was enough to put off the rest. The big black and the limping gray seemed especially wary; they stood on the skyline, looking down. Then they were gone.

As I trudged back to camp, I kicked myself for not staying put. Then again, maybe the pack wouldn't have come any closer. I'd never know, but this much was true: we'd each taken steps toward the other, emissaries from alien species, and something like peace had passed between us. The gray wolf's stick had seemed a gesture of trust, even an offer of play.

Back in Ambler, old Nelson Greist would shake his head and laugh at my earnest explanation. "Maybe they try to eat you," he said. "You just never know it."

Traveling with My Eyes

❖

I looked out across the valley, wondering where
they'd gone. In just ten minutes, I'd gone from
riches—a dozen wolves on the edge of camp, the
nearest one just forty yards away—to nothing. The
pack had vanished, and I knew they wouldn't be back.
As Clarence might say, I'd used up my luck.

I tried to shrug off my disappointment, the feeling
that something more should have happened, and went
back to what I'd come for. There were sheep on the
mountain above, and I hoped to find one for spring
meat. I was a fool to ask for more than what lay

before me: the upper Noatak on a perfect late April day, the snow collapsing in hisses, the promise of five days here alone.

Seven hours later, I pulled into camp. I'd found a big ram below the first cliff—an easy stalk, a clean kill, a rough but short pack out—and spent the rest of the afternoon quietly, walking the ridge, sitting in the sun as lambs and ewes grazed just a few yards away. Far below, the Noatak's serpentine loops glinted blue and green, filling with meltwater. Several times I crossed fresh trails left by other predators—wolf, grizzly, wolverine—all hunting the same mountain, hoping for the same thing. I headed back at twilight, snow crisping in the wind.

I was sorting gear outside the tent when I heard wolves again. This time they were below me, out on the flats. Setting up my spotting scope, I found them—one gray here, two there, then a black, a half mile off, curled up on the snow. As I watched, one raised its muzzle to the sky, and another answered.

Then I saw the birds, two ravens squatting by a dark, circular depression nearby. One wolf rose, stretched, and limped toward them: the crippled gray I'd seen last night. Not only had the pack not cleared out, they were napping within plain sight of my tent.

The cripple settled less than ten feet from the birds, who scarcely ruffled a feather. The three sat there like old men on a park bench, trading stories. I'd seen ravens following wolves, scavenging kills; biologists report the two species hunting, even playing together. Still, seeing them so close together, so relaxed, seemed like something out of Disney.

Another wolf sauntered over and began digging and tugging. I could just make out a caribou antler, rising like a clawed hand from the snow. The black wolf rose and, without a glance in my direction, joined the others.

I knew, at that point, that I was staying put. I'd planned on riding up Midas Creek into the Nigu, maybe doubling back through Portage Creek, but that one hundred fifty miles of country, spectacular as it was, would have to wait. More than I'd ever hoped to see was here, on this rather ordinary stretch of tundra, caught between the curve of treeless, ragged mountains. I'd travel with my eyes instead.

I still figured the pack would move on. They'd moved less than a mile in two days, a fraction of their territory. But when I sat down to the scope the next morning, I found wolves again. I'd studied this patch of country enough, by now, to tune into slight changes—to find, say, a sleeping wolf curled up against a clump of brush a thousand yards away. And knowing they were there kept me looking.

Though I'd originally seen twelve, now I counted only seven. They'd split up, not an unusual event. Though a pack is a close-knit family, they often separate into smaller groups or singles, ranging far to travel and hunt—twenty, fifty, sometimes a hundred miles, before reuniting.

Over the next two days, wolves floated like smoke across the sweep of tundra before me. From my vantage point on the knoll, with my 15- to 60-power scope, I commanded nearly a square mile, from the northern rim of the valley to the high bluffs that drop to the Noatak River. Between my camp and the river was a stairstep series of lakes, following the slope from mountains to river. Though from here the terrain looked smooth, there were dozens of creases and undulations, each enough to hide a hundred wolves. Following these conduits, they often appeared out of nowhere and vanished just as abruptly, moving at a brisk, steady trot that seemed both weightless and tireless. One minute wolves seemed to be everywhere; then the flats would fall silent, sometimes for hours. Each time I thought they were gone for good. Then a howl would drift up on the wind, and I'd know.

The old frozen-in caribou carcass was a rendezvous. They took turns digging, but didn't seem too serious, nor especially hungry. Bored was more like it. They napped, wandered, parted, and converged. Now and then I saw one stiffen, then pounce, paws bunched, trying to pin a vole under the snow.

They howled more than any pack I'd ever encountered, sometimes for minutes at a stretch, and sporadically all day and night. One young gray in particular (a female, I guessed) seemed to love making a racket. She would trot from wolf to wolf, coax others to join in, then continue long after her pack-mates had wandered off, disgusted. Often she sang alone, a thin, quavering yodel I learned to recognize. For obvious reasons, I labeled her the howler.

But I resisted the urge to name them; that seemed an act of ownership, or a claim of false familiarity. I was a voyeur peering in their windows, hoping to witness the intimate details of their lives. I'm sure they had no name for me. I was that loud, odiferous, somewhat puzzling but inconsequential creature on the hill over there. They gave no sign of knowing that I had the power to roar down on them like a Valkyrie, rifle flashing.

I never knew if they were trusting, brave, or merely indifferent. The wolves remained, for all my prying, inscrutable as creatures from another galaxy. As I sat and watched in the deepening twilight, I found myself offering them a wordless prayer, a simple thanks for not knowing, or maybe caring, who I was.

Permission

The seven wolves milled around on the tundra below me, drifting in and out of sight. Without a fresh kill to hold the pack here, I was down to one explanation. The black wolf was about to have pups. It was exactly the time of year. I suspected the den lay between here and the Noatak River, nestled into a sandy bluff.

I'd stumbled on the sort of chance that many biologists never get in an entire career. Most wolf studies involve radio collars, dissections, airplane tracking, habituated, even fenced animals. Here was a pack of wild wolves, going about their business out in plain sight. I jotted notes on slabs of cardboard when my paper gave out, and leaned against the eyepiece of my beat-up scope until my vision blurred. I wasn't driven by anything as altruistic as scientific curiosity. I was more like an amateur detective who'd worked a case for years, always a step behind, then finally caught up.

I'd stood three paces from a grizzly, pulled back my feet so caribou wouldn't step on them, stroked the wet ears of a newborn moose calf. Nothing compared with what I saw now, as I sat drinking coffee ten feet from my tent. The wolves passed around my camp as if it were a strange outcropping that had always been there, part of the landscape. It all seemed like a waking dream.

As I began to recognize individuals in the pack, a social order emerged. The black wolf and a big brown-gray male were in charge. Then there was the cripple, who was always the first to notice me if I edged closer. The other four grays were almost identical, last spring's litter, I figured, the sometimes foolish, inquisitive wolves that biologists call pups of the year. The howler was one of these. So were the two wolves who'd approached camp the first morning.

The big brown-gray male was the pack bully. He'd trot up to the young wolves as they napped and stand stiff-legged over each, reminding them, in wolf language, who was boss. Once I saw him throw a shoulder into the howler, bowl her over, and snatch away a scrap of caribou hide, just because he could. The younger wolf cringed, then slunk off, head down, tail tucked, an almost comical picture of dejection.

The big male, along with the others, showed deference to the black wolf—the alpha female, I guessed. They all fawned, wagged tails, and seemed to beg her favor.

Watching the pack interact was like eavesdropping on an animated conversation in Swahili. There was obviously a great deal being said—complex, coordinated movements would often follow a simple stare or a round of nose-touching—but I could do little more than guess the actual content. I thought I knew something about wolves, but now I realized how small that something was.

Of course, I wasn't satisfied. Though I felt self-righteous about my own peaceful intentions—the wolves I'd hunted and shot in the past seemed a distant bad dream—the truth was, I still wanted something from them. The biggest camera lens I had along was a 200. That meant getting inside fifty yards if I wanted something good.

On the third evening, with a red sun hanging low against the hills, I drove slowly, quietly as I could, straight for the old caribou kill. The black, the cripple, and three of the young grays had gathered there again, wagging tails and digging at the frozen-in carcass. Without cover, across a half mile of kneedeep slush, I figured a direct approach was as good a bet as any. The machine rattled beneath me, huge in the stillness.

The cripple bolted before I'd covered a quarter mile, followed by the black wolf and two of the grays. Oh well, I thought. I hadn't really expected this to work.

But the last wolf didn't run. He waited alone as I idled toward him. I stopped fifty yards away, and he approached, tail held low, but slightly out—a gesture that showed he, at least, was relaxed. I lifted my camera, braced my shaking arms on the windshield, and shot off two rolls of film against the setting sun.

The wolf kept edging in, circling downwind. Now I could see his eyes, the quiver of his nose as he tested the air. I thought I recognized him as the young gray who'd approached camp the first morning, but I couldn't be sure. I only knew I'd never hoped to get this close.

Maybe too close. A wave of unease washed over my elation. What was between me and a jaw-snapping rush? A foolish fear, maybe, but real all the same. And what about the wolf? Did I want him to approach the next snowmobile he saw, Clarence's maybe? I hesitated, then gunned my machine toward him.

He seemed shocked, totally nonplussed. Leaping aside, he trotted off a few steps, looking over his shoulder. I made another pass, and this time he understood. Head low, tail out, he ran as only a wolf can run, a blur that vanished into the twilight.

After that, I didn't crowd them. In return, the wolves offered me more than I deserved, more than I'd given: permission to simply be, without question or conflict. I kept imagining the faint roar of approaching hunters, and each time I felt a surge of panic. But the wolves hadn't asked me to be their keeper, and I had to trust them to find their own way in a world where so many wanted something from them—their hides, pictures, maybe just a glimpse.

In the evening cool I packed my sled. After three straight days of sun, breakup was booming out of the hills. If I waited another day, I might be trapped on the north side of the valley, one hundred twenty-five miles from home. A last look through the scope revealed nothing. But as I tied down my load, a lone howl rose from the flats. I returned a silent good-bye.

The Song of Ice

❖

I stand with old Shield Downey, looking downhill toward the frozen Kobuk River. "When will it break up?" I ask. "I don't know," shrugs Shield. All around Ambler, people are asking each other the same thing. It's the end of May, and the ice should have moved by now. In the arctic, blizzards and twenty below zero can last through April, but the elders say they've never seen breakup come this late. The willows should be green, and the *Iviisaapaatmiut* out boating, hunting beaver and ducks. Instead, the snow lies three feet deep, and we've just had a few inches more. Some say it's the endless winter the Eskimo prophet Maniilaq predicted a century ago.

There are a few hopeful tokens: patches of open water and dark streaks along the Kobuk's banks show that the current is steadily gnawing upward, the water rising. The caribou, too, have been pouring north, and the rusty cries of sandhill cranes echo across the tundra. Late afternoon temperatures are enough to send meltwater gushing down gullies under the snow, but the ice in front of town is still four feet thick, solid beneath a foot of slush, and shows no sign of budging.

Meanwhile, everyone's trapped. Except in the frosty evenings, when a few hunters splash their snowmobiles across the tundra in search of geese, travel in the country is impossible. After the wide freedom of March and April, the long, snow-bright days that the Inupiat call "springtime," there is suddenly nowhere to go. Breakup, like the autumn freeze, is a time of waiting, of still, dreamlike days. A few people work half-heartedly on their boats—overhauling outboards, patching worn keels—but a glance at the frozen river makes that seem absurd. Even to those who have seen the ice go dozens of times, waiting is an act of faith.

June opens sun-drenched, the clouds gone at last, and a few pans of ice have broken free in front of the fish racks. People look toward the river and nod. "Any time now," the elders say. There's an ice jam a mile below town, another at the hairpin bend just above us—blue and white slabs of ice three to five feet thick crushed into twisted piles higher than a man can reach. And behind the jam there are two hundred miles of ice waiting upstream, creaking and shifting as the Kobuk rises.

Several times a day I walk down the hill, drawn by the simple miracle of moving water; after seven months of stiff white silence, the river's swirling rush, two hundred yards of open current in front of town, is mesmerizing. Two days ago was too early, but now I remember what's coming: the explosion of green, clouds of mosquitoes, the splash of grayling, the glitter of stones in water so pure it seems like air.

I'm sitting in my cabin at 2 A.M.—not quite bedtime in these days of endless light—when I decide to check once more. I pull on my jacket and trot down the hill toward the river. The sun has dipped behind the Jade Mountains, and mist rises from the Kobuk as it pours by, smooth and silver in the half-light. There are no geese calling, not a breath of wind; far across the flats to the east, the mountains seem like painted images, too sharply etched to be real. I lean against a birch and drift off with the river, forgetting that I'd planned to stay only a few minutes.

A faint rumble stirs the silence. I wonder if I've imagined it, but then there's another, and a low, steady roar gathers, grows into a crescendo of crashing and grinding as if the hills were wrenching open. The jam just above town has let go—a surging jumble of white, thousands of tons of pressure bursting free, piling around the bend with startling speed. Spruce on the far bank sway, and one splinters as a train-sized wedge of ice rams the bank, breaches, and falls back, carrying the tree with it. From downstream a shout rings out, "Ice go! Ice go!" and I know I wasn't waiting alone.

Suddenly the river's edge swarms with activity—kids shouting and throwing stones, teenagers on four-wheelers, older people standing together—all gathered on the high bank to watch the wreckage of winter churn past. This day, more than any other, marks the passage of a season. The winter has lasted eight months—months of darkness and sixty below zero, days of storms and nights drifting with ice fog. Now, as we watch, one door swings shut, another opens. Arctic summer is here.

A gunshot crashes out, then a dozen more. Young men are shooting over the water as they have for generations, honoring the belief that gunfire helps the ice pass quickly. Other people scramble to move boats and fish racks to higher ground; no longer choked by ice jams, the Kobuk is rising by the minute. In some years the muddy water stops inches short of the lowest houses. Although my own boat is pulled twenty feet above the present waterline, I know I might have to move it higher.

Logs, tangles of brush, oil drums, and a wrecked boat whirl past, caught in the crush of ice. Floes the size of parking lots grind and slam against each other, and countless smaller chunks jostle and tumble; some are sucked under and obliterated, others shoved onto the bank, where they lie stranded like crystal whales. Part of me wants to jump on a big chunk and ride whooping around the bend, though I know a man couldn't last a minute if things went wrong.

The voice of flowing ice, though not thunderous, fills the

air—thousands of individual sounds interwoven, a dense texture that seems to come from everywhere, and to be the sound of everything: the rumble of machinery, the roar of distant surf, the murmur of crowds, the hiss of space. And beneath it all is music—a delicate, liquid shattering, a song of returning, of breathing again after long silence. I should join the others in their celebration, but just now I want to sit alone, to watch and listen as the winter breaks apart.

Fourteen Bucks

❖

The Twin Otter drones out of the Brooks Range, five hundred feet over the Anaktuvuk River. Below, the winter tundra glows in the morning light. We point to bands of grazing caribou; moose hunker in the willows, dark against the snow. There are seven of us pressing our noses to the cold glass, watching the land unfurl, three Native, four white. This million-dollar plane was sent just for us. We're guests of the Atlantic Richfield Company, headed for a VIP tour of Prudhoe Bay.

Any Alaskan knows what Prudhoe is all about.

Eighty-five percent of all state revenues flows from oil, and the biggest working fields—Prudhoe, Kuparuk, Lisburne, Endicott—are on the North Slope, the sixty-mile-wide plain bordering the Beaufort Sea. But few people outside the industry ever see the place it all comes from. Traffic on the Dalton Highway, also known as the haul road, is restricted, and the jet fare to Deadhorse (an adjoining commercial enclave open to the public) is steep. Either way, you're still outside the ARCO and BP checkpoints, looking in. Unless you're part of a tour, or you know somebody, that's as far as you go.

I just happened to be at the right place at the right time. Once a year, ARCO offers a tour to the staff of each North Slope village school, part of an ongoing public relations program; I was visiting the *Nunamiut* school in Anaktuvuk Pass when their turn came, and I grabbed the chance.

The Otter banks, and there, sprawled to the horizon, are jumbles of modular buildings, the glint of metal and machinery, miles of pipeline and connecting roads. Spread out on this windswept plain, where single caribou stand out as if spotlit, the sudden appearance of all this man-made clutter is startling, its scope overwhelming. I don't know what I'd expected. Maybe I'd imagined that the oil fields themselves would be more compressed, more aesthetically pleasing.

But Prudhoe is the largest oil field in North America, and it looks like what it is. There's nothing pretty about modular industrial construction on this scale. Twenty-five billion dollars have been invested, and over a million barrels of oil and gas are pumped from the ground every day. Together, the six producing North Slope fields cover roughly five hundred square miles. This is big business with an exclamation point, and I have no right to expect anything different. Like everybody else in Alaska, I depend on the oil industry, even if I don't like admitting it.

Without state oil money, my home village of Ambler would hardly exist. As in most bush villages, there's not much in the way of a local economy, let alone a tax base. Subsistence hunting and fishing is a way of life, but it doesn't bring in money. Yet we have electricity, water and sewer, an airport with state-of-the-art navigational aids, a cold storage plant, satellite relays for phone and TV, prefabricated houses, a clinic, and a two-million-dollar school—all partially or totally funded by our share of the huge oil revenue pie. Even my teaching salary, like most salaries here (from city manager to power plant operator), flows straight down the pipeline.

Inside the ARCO base camp building, Oliver Smith greets us like old pals. It's his job to show us around, and he clearly enjoys his work. Inside ten minutes, he's memorized all of our names. We start off with a basic orientation—glossy brochures, a slide show, questions and answers over coffee. The conference room is comfortable, like the entire facility. ARCO offers its workers art exhibits, a movie theater, a health club, lounges, wide-screen TVs, dining areas decorated with green plants and featuring lavish menus. Today's brunch includes eggs Benedict, deep-fried catfish, and chicken fajitas.

As Oliver explains the ABCs of oil, everything from injection technology to spill response, I can't help but be impressed by his eloquence and charm. Sure, he has his spiel down, but it's more than acting. He has the power of conviction behind his words, genuine enthusiasm for this grand industrial adventure and his part in it. ARCO seems a benevolent force toiling for the common good, heedless of profit or expense. My embossed, souvenir-quality visitor's nametag bears additional information: ARCO SAFE; OPEN ANWR, AMERICA'S ENERGY FUTURE.

Outside, it's a typical February day in Prudhoe: twenty below, and a bitter east wind sweeping off the ice. We're herded onto a bus driven by a uniformed, pistol-toting security guard. As we thread along the geometric, seemingly endless maze of roads, Oliver keeps up his patter. Here is a cluster of "Christmas trees," the elaborate fireplugs that cap producing wells; there, a flow station, where gas and water are removed from crude oil. Far across the tundra, surreal in the ice fog, are drill sites, separation centers, a gas plant. And everywhere flow the bright metal veins of pipeline, connecting it all.

Something is making me edgy, adding to the strangeness. At first I can't place what's wrong, and then I realize: no people. Hardly any trucks moving. All these buildings, and no one in sight. We might as well be touring the industrial parks of Mars. "There's only about four hundred ARCO employees left up here," says Oliver. "Oil production's declining, and everything's automated. Right now, we have more vehicles than people."

At Flow Station Three, we see what he means. This tangle of pipes, pumps, and valves, the size of several football fields, is all run from a computerized control room, where a few technicians ride herd on banks of flashing lights. The huge, dim corridors are empty, silent except for the hum of machinery. Rachel Riley, one of the Inupiat instructors, leans over and whispers, "Does something feel funny around here, or is it just me?"

"Think of it this way," says Oliver Smith, gesturing toward a four-foot pipe overhead. "Today's price for North Slope crude is $14.16 a barrel. Snap your fingers like this"—his cadence is around twice a second—"and say to yourself, 'fourteen bucks, fourteen bucks, fourteen bucks.' That's how much money's going down that line."

It's an infectious way of thinking. On the bus, and on the plane back to Anaktuvuk Pass, and for days afterward, I hear people snapping their fingers along with Oliver. Fourteen bucks, fourteen bucks.

The Quiet Voices

Every afternoon Shield Downey would be there, sitting on his porch steps across from the Ambler post office. Some people would nod or wave, but few stopped to talk. Still, the old widower would sit outside, bundled against the cold, watching everyone come and go.

I paused once in a while. We'd talk about the weather, or I'd tell him where I'd been out in the country, what I'd seen. His face would light up then; as a young man, he'd traveled with dogs to the same places. He couldn't do much now, he said, pointing to a hernia bulging through his parka, as if apologizing for his failing body. Now and then I'd bring him a fat young beaver or a trout heavy with eggs—delicacies I knew he craved and couldn't get for himself.

Though I knew Shield for ten years, we never got past a simple, superficial friendship. I was never quite sure what to talk about, and though I wanted to know the story of his life, asking too many questions seemed an intrusion. I thought, too, that there would be time ahead to know each other. I was always tired, or I was busy—a story to write, wood to chop, a trip somewhere. I kept putting it off.

Then he was gone. I wasn't even in town when he died. If I'd been an Eskimo, I would have dropped everything, walked out on my job, and flown home for the funeral. But I knew it was too late to make a gesture.

They keep dying. Old Maude Foxgloves with her cane and goose-wing fan, squinting in the summer sun; Mark Cleveland, garrulous and outgoing, with his sly sense of humor; Nellie Woods, bent double by arthritis, beaming as she dragged her sled down to the river to fish at ten below zero. There were others: Louie and Annie Commack, Mabel Walton, Walter Downey, Emma Porter, David Adams, Elsie Douglas, and now Bessie Douglas and Ned Howarth...all friends or neighbors from Noatak and Ambler, all Inupiat elders I knew. Across the region, dozens more have died, one by one: in Buckland, Selawik, Shungnak, or in hospital beds far to the south.

These people lived full, rich lives, many into their eighties.

They sewed skins, hunted, carved, and cut fish until they were no longer able. In their younger days they lived with the land, traveling between camps by dog teams and kayak, surviving blizzards, taking pleasure in small things: a sunset, a warm fire, a good marrowbone. Some, like Mark Cleveland, lived to hold thirty grandchildren. How can I mourn? I've spent too many years among hunters and gatherers to deny death its season. Yet I think of Shield Downey, whom I barely knew, and feel like crying.

It's not the death of elders I mourn. It's what's dying with them, and what's taking their place. I look around Ambler, or any Native village, and see the prefabricated "housings" go up in neat rows, the satellite dishes that bring CNN and the Disney Channel, the carpeted schools with banks of computers, the pop cans and candy wrappers. Just a century ago, the first white explorers came into the upper Kobuk valley. The people they found, the *Kuuvanjmiut*, still used spears, wore skins, and thought that being rich meant a cache full of meat.

Some I knew, like Walter Downey from Noatak, were young enough to watch it all happen: guns for bows and arrows, trade cloth for pelts, then outboard motors, airplanes, semiautomatic carbines. It hasn't been that long. If I'd gotten up here just fifteen years earlier than I did, I'd have seen Ambler's first snowmobile. I just missed the first telephones and television. Now the kids I teach—the grandchildren of Mark, Emma, Annie, and Shield—wear starter jackets, listen to rap, and idolize Michael Jordan. When they think of being rich, they see Porsches and swimming pools. A cultural McDonald's looms on the horizon.

The old ways were hardly idyllic. I remember Mark Cleveland laughing when I asked him if he wanted to go back. "Too hard," he said, shaking his head. "Things are easier now. Better." The equation of easier with better isn't hard to figure when you hear the stories. Starvation in hard times was sometimes part of life, along with spiritual terrorism by corrupt *anjatkut*, or shamans. There was constant moving between camps; the weak might be left to die. Even helping a woman in childbirth was taboo. Along came the missionaries and traders, offering both a material and spiritual way out. It's not surprising that The People accepted, no doubt believing that they could take what they needed and leave the rest. That's how life had always been.

Now the elders look out, bemused, at a world that's left them behind. Once, old age guaranteed status; children wouldn't dream of disobedience or rudeness. Though a great deal of lip service is paid, and "respect for elders" is the foremost command in a list of official cultural values labeled *Inupiat Ilitquisiat*, the old people don't have any real power. City councils, school boards, and Native corporations rule Alaskan bush politics. Beyond lies a bureaucratic tangle of state and federal agencies, controlling everything from building projects to land use. True, each village has its elders council, and there are regional conferences from time to time. Schools have Inupiat Days, when the elders are invited to speak or teach skills.

But the old people, the last who remember what it was to be real Inupiat, are little more than figureheads, relegated to talking about the good old days, setting down remembrances on tape, occasionally administering a public scolding. All too often they're drowned out by the roar of machines, the television's racket, the endless basketball games at the gym. There are simply too many distractions, and the quiet voices go unheard.

You'd expect them to be bitter, but there's seldom a trace. The elders go about their lives with the serenity of people certain who they are. Though so much has changed, the land is still there, offering its gifts: fish to net, berries and birchbark to gather, caribou crossing downstream—the same things that made life good when they were young, that made them Inupiat. I look at the smiling faces of these people, my friends who still live, grateful for so much, asking for so little. How can I mourn when they refuse?

This Place

❖

I sit outside my tent, drinking coffee and looking back where I've been. The Ipnelivik valley slides into shadows, but the highest peaks are brilliantly lit, ridges of dark rock and snow reflecting light so pure I can see a grizzly's tracks far up a slope more than a mile away. I can see, too, the curve of my own trail, and where the two intersected.

Two hours ago I met him, a big male just out of his winter den. I'd been following his sign up the canyon, and there he was, standing on a crag a hundred yards above, peering down, waiting for me.

I shut off my snowmachine. He cocked his head, testing the air. Then, with a huff, he bounded uphill. When I circled back I could see him, a thousand feet higher now and headed for the skyline. He wasn't in any hurry—just going up the mountain and over the top, into the Ingning valley. I watched him dwindle to a black speck against the snow, tried to concentrate so I'd remember forty years from now. This bear. This place. This day.

I've come here alone, over a hundred miles with snowmachine and sled, climbing out of the Kobuk valley through Ivisaaq Pass, winding my way into the windswept upper Noatak, traveling without any certain plan or destination. I do this once a year in late March or early April: drop whatever else I'm doing—job, writing, chores—pack my sled, and head north into the Brooks Range. By the time I return, I'll have covered four hundred miles.

Some Ambler people shake their heads, wondering what I'm up to. It's not safe, they say. It might get stormy. You could freeze. What if you break down?

Back in camp, my pocket thermometer reads nine above zero, and the night wind falls down the valley. The temperature has dropped twenty degrees since afternoon, and may drop another twenty, though the sky is suffused with a pale glow. The snow lies chest-deep in the willows, but this season, which the Inupiat call springtime, is defined by light. The days grow longer by seven, then ten minutes, the pace intoxicating after the numb darkness of winter. By mid-April the sun hardly sets.

You can feel spring gathering itself, waiting to explode green and warm, alive with the cackle of geese, the whistle of snipe, and everywhere the crash of meltwater rushing for the sea.

I've pitched my canvas tent against a sheltering patch of brush. Digging a couple of feet into the snow, I've packed down a floor overlaid with willow branches, tarp, and a caribou-skin sleeping pad. Heat comes from a sheet-metal woodstove fed with scrub willow. A clutter of drying gear hangs along the ridgepole; my sleeping bags are rolled against the back wall. An Eskimo from another century would recognize what I'm up to.

Outside, the rest of my gear—gas cans, grub box, rifle, spare parts, tools, clothes duffel—is heaped in the twelve-foot basket sled, covered with a tarp. My snowmachine, a battered Arctic Cat, rests under a coat of frost. The whole setup doesn't look like much, but it's simple and tough. It works.

Dinner, like my gear, is nothing fancy: a pan full of Rice-A-Roni with extra margarine and cheese, chased by two quarts of tea, crackers, and a frozen can of peaches. Eating right in cold weather, a diet heavy in fat, carbohydrate, and fluid, is just as important as the right parka.

After filling the stove one last time, I hang my clothes, layers of polypropylene, fleece, and nylon, and switch into dry sleeping gear. Nestled in two down bags, I listen to the stove's hiss and wait for sleep. But when I close my eyes, I find I've been filled with brightness. All I've seen today comes back.

I could tell you where I was with map and compass, an orderly list of facts. Put this way, it's all clear enough: I traveled with snowmachine up the east fork of the Ipnelivik on an April morning, and made it almost as far as Blind Pass, where I ran into overflow and turned back. The mountains were jagged and white, the sky deep blue. I saw where a gyrfalcon had hit a ptarmigan and left bones, feathers, and wingprints scattered on the crest of a knoll. I followed fresh wolverine tracks, and traced the week-old meandering of a young grizzly to a side canyon so narrow the rocks almost touched overhead. Turning up the Ipnelivik's west branch, I rode through unmarked powder to the base of an arête, where I ate lunch, played harmonica, and listened to the snow melt.

Over the course of the day, I shot several rolls of film, picked up a sunburn, and got my machine stuck a few times. In the long shadows of evening, heading home, I cut a fresh grizzly trail, followed it, and caught a glimpse of its maker.

All this tells where I've been, but explains nothing. It doesn't tell you that kneeling before the falcon's kill, I wept; that as I rode, I laughed aloud, and often stopped to raise my arms to the sky, not knowing what else to do; that I took fifty photos of the same peak in shifting light; that when I played harmonica, it was for the mountains, as if they could hear.

It's been four years, now. I look back, vaguely embarrassed, as I would have been if someone had seen me that day. I can't tell you that my heart left my body and came back filled with light, or that I forgot, for a time, where the land ended and I began, even if it's true. Words, like map and compass, tell one story but fail at another, just as when I sorted through the fifty slides I took of that mountain and ended up throwing most out. The ones I kept were fine—sharp focus, good composition, proper exposure—but the thing I'd tried to hold had slipped away.

I've been back to the Ipnelivik since, and it's still good country, some of the best I've seen. The mountains remain, bathed in light, and bears roam through silent canyons where the rocks almost meet overhead. But the place I seek is somewhere else, now—just over the next ridge, or the one beyond. I ride out, hoping.

ABOUT THE AUTHOR

Nick Jans is one of Alaska's most recognized and prolific writers. A contributing editor to *ALASKA* magazine and a member of *USA Today's* board of editorial contributors, he's written nine books and hundreds of magazine articles. Jans has also been the recipient of numerous writing awards, most recently two Ben Franklin Medals (2007 and 2008). He currently lives in Juneau with his wife, Sherrie, and travels widely in Alaska. He returns each year to Ambler, the arctic Inupiaq village he still calls "home."

Printed in the USA
CPSIA information can be obtained
at www.ICGtesting.com
JSHW012030140824
68134JS00033B/2970

9 780882 408071